She Fulfilled the Impossible Dream

The Story of Eva B. Dykes

She

The Story of Eva B. Dykes

Fulfilled the Impossible Dream

DeWitt S. Williams

11811

REVIEW AND HERALD® PUBLISHING ASSOCIATION
HAGERSTOWN, MD 21740

1. Dykes, Eva Beatrice, 1893-1986. 2. Seventh-day
Adventists—United States—Biography. 3. College
teachers—United States—Biography. I. Title.
BX6193.D94W54 1985 286.7'32' 0924 [B] 84-17726

Contents

Dedication

I dedicate this book to my wife, who, as an outstanding teacher, follows in the tradition of Eva B. Dykes. I would like to thank the many people who gave of their time and comments to make this book possible: Esther Osborne Ward; Agnes Barksdale, Dr. Dykes' cousin; contemporary friends Helen Sugland, Joe and Willie Dodson, Myrtle G. Murphy, Alan and Lucille Anderson, and Lillian Burges Ashby; Mary Rose Allen, former teacher with Eva B. Dykes at Howard University; and Jannith Lewis, who made available resource materials from the Eva B. Dykes Library at Oakwood College.

I would also like to thank the authors of previously written articles about Eva Dykes. I do not include footnotes in the story, but admit that I had to depend heavily on their information and research to make my story complete. Most helpful were "The Achievements of Eva Beatrice Dykes," by Lela M. Gooding; *Climbing High Mountains,* by F. L. Peterson; "She Fulfilled the Impossible Dream," by Louis B. Reynolds; Jannith Lewis' 1973 unpublished interview with Dr. Dykes on civil rights; Clara Rock's March, 1975, interview with Dr. Dykes, also unpublished; "A Glimpse at Dr. Eva B. Dykes," by Gwen Ward; and the article "Dr. Eva Beatrice Dykes," prepared for *Spectrum* by Irene

Wakeham but unpublished.

Most sincere appreciation goes to all of the cooperative people at Howard University for opening up their rich resources: Jane S. Knowles, Radcliffe College archivist; Lona Nell Lea and C. D. Brooks, for helpful suggestions; Debra M. Carroll, for typing, editing, and retyping the manuscript; and my family, for patiently enduring the odd and unusually long hours that I spent at my desk and away from them while writing this book. Last, but not least, to Dr. Eva B. Dykes herself, who patiently answered my myriad questions.

The Challenge

E va Beatrice Dykes!"
    Hearing her name, she lifted her head and walked briskly to the center of the stage. Polite applause could not hide the spontaneous murmur that spread throughout the all-white audience.

"Isn't that a colored girl?" Those in the back rows stretched their necks to see, while those in the front stared in unbelief. But all whispered the same question. "Isn't that a colored girl?"

Undaunted, she took the diploma and pumped the outstretched hand. "Thank you. Thank you very much," she managed to say.

Flicking her tassel to the other side of her mortarboard, she continued to the spot where the seven female doctoral candidates were to stand. Commencement day, June 22, 1921, was different from any that had gone before. Since it opened its doors in 1879, Radcliffe, an exclusive, Ivy-League college for women, had not conferred this highest honor on a black person.

She stood with humble dignity, representing not one but two minority groups. Black women in America have always faced the double obstacles of gender and race to achieve their dreams and aspirations. That so many have succeeded in so many varied fields is a testament to their strength.

Her presence silently proclaimed that her skin, though black, covered a brain that could think as clearly and reason as profoundly as that of the fairest white. She also testified that those of the so-called weaker sex were mentally as strong and alert as their male counterparts at nearby Harvard—or at any university, for that matter. Although tiny in stature, she was a lady giant.

Her slave grandparents had held hoes in their hands to cultivate cotton. Now her hands held a diploma. That piece of paper showing she had earned a doctorate in English could be the magic key that she could use to obtain fame and recognition. It could open the door to financial success and wealth. Now she could teach in any school in the United States that had the good sense not to bar her because of her race. Her diploma could bring her into contact with the intellectual elite of the nation, black or white.

But long before her graduation she had decided that she would dedicate herself to service in the black community. To be great, to be first, was not her goal. Rather, to be her best so that she could render the best service and uplift humanity and her God had been her aim.

The formalities over, she rushed to the big house where she roomed and boarded. The dormitories did not yet accept black students and she had been advised to find a room in the nearby community of Cambridge, Massachusetts.

"My family will be waiting for me at the train station," she said to temperamental Bess, the owner of the house where she boarded.

"Goodbye, Eva. We're proud of you." Bess would really miss the young graduate student. Then Eva ran by quickly to see Sio An Chu, a Chinese girl. Each represented a minority at Radcliffe, and they had become close friends. They embraced in farewell.

Eva's days at Radcliffe had been full, busy, and pleasant. Although her teachers supported and inspired her, and although they manifested no real, overt prejudice, there existed an air of reserve. It had been a challenge to enroll, to compete, and to graduate from Radcliffe.

Dr. James Howard drummed his fingers on his desk. His body sat in Washington, D.C., but his mind was in Cambridge, Massachusetts. Once again he regretted that his busy schedule had prevented him from attending his beloved niece's graduation. If it had been on the weekend, he could have arranged something. But a Wednesday graduation was out of the question.

If only two o'clock would come. Her train was scheduled to arrive that afternoon, and he wanted her to know how proud he was. The pace of his fingers speeded up, trying to rush the seconds by.

"Martha! Are you ready? Is Anita ready? We should leave in one hour so we can get to the train station on time. We don't want Eva to wait in the hot sun too long."

His voice, slightly edged with impatience, had the unmistakable ring of culture and education. He had received his B.A. from Howard University's College of Liberal Arts in 1879, and the M.D. degree from Howard's School of Medicine in 1883. In 1885 he became the fifth student of the Howard University Liberal Arts College to earn a Master of Arts degree. James Howard was so well respected that even his sister, Martha, and his nieces and close friends called him "Doctor."

"Doctor, we'll be ready. Just you wait and see," his sister replied. Though fragile and sickly, she had surprising energy. She pushed herself and her family of three girls to keep the physician's eight-room home spotless. The house, at 1724 Eighth Street NW., Washington, D.C., was the pride of the neighborhood.

The train ride from Cambridge to Washington proved uneventful to Eva. The seats around her were unoccupied, and she had ample opportunity to reflect. The *clickety-clack* of the wheels on the rails made her think of another train ride seven years earlier, in 1914. That time she was leaving Washington, headed for Nashville, Tennessee. She had just earned her B.A. at Howard, summa cum laude, and had accepted a call to Walden University, a struggling little black school not now in existence.

She remembered how she and other black riders packed a small Jim Crow car directly behind the locomotive. The indignity of the situation caused more tears than the soot and cinders that bombarded her eyes and face. No one cared that she had been valedictorian and had won the Alpha Kappa Alpha Scholastic Award. At that time no other Howard graduate had left its campus with a summa cum laude.

After a round of introductions and small talk, two black women in the car discovered that Eva was going to Walden to teach Latin and English.

"You gonna try to teach them boneheads some Latin? Northern English and literature?"

"They need to know how to build houses, them men does."

"Women need to learn how to cook, clean, and take care of babies." A long laugh.

"What's English, Latin, and literature gonna do?" More laughter. "Women need to know 'bout church, chores, and children."

Eva replied rather eruditely, "When looked at quickly, literature doesn't seem to stand up as a very practical subject. Certainly one doesn't construct a building with a degree in English, but literature has its value in its *message*. Literature helps a people's spirit and helps preserve the language.

"It can be very practical, too. I know it can change a reader's attitude, and even alter his behavior." Unimpressed, her new acquaintances continued to smirk and whisper until they got off at their stop.

Depressed, Eva almost left the train at the next stop, ready to return to Washington. Had she chosen correctly? She could work in the nation's capital. Even then she was qualified to rub shoulders with the intelligentsia of government and academia. Why be subjected to indignities such as this? But she remembered the words printed in the Howard University *Record* that commented on her student life and career goals:

"But Miss Dykes was a different type of student. From the beginning, she approached her work with a totally different emphasis, and with all that she has acquired, she has lost none of those admirable traits of character that are necessary for the successful man or woman.

"In disposition and training she is peculiarly well-qualified for a brilliant career of usefulness." *Usefulness.* She remembered that word and that phrase. "Peculiarly well-qualified for a brilliant career of usefulness."

"I must go to Walden. They need me there, and I must go." Brushing the soot from her dress and hair, she wiped her eyes with a handkerchief and braced herself for the rest of the trip and the beginning of a life of usefulness and service in the black community.

As Eva now rode south from Cambridge she remembered Walden, her first teaching assignment, her first real commitment to a life of useful service to her people. She thought of the many students she had given not only the tools to express themselves but also an appreciation for their mother tongue.

Also she remembered that her salary of $24 a month plus room and board never seemed to allow her to buy the special literature books that she liked to read. But the experience was beyond value. Memories of it flooded back. Every morning, before she got out of bed, she would hear a knock. One of the students had arrived to stir the fire in the fireplace to make the room comfortable for her. That first year of teaching had left her with such pleasant experiences.

The train slowed now. The screech of wheels against rails pulled her out of her reverie. She had reached Washington.

"I hope Doctor brought the family to meet me." After she waited for several men in front of her to get off, she picked up her two suitcases and climbed down.

At first they couldn't see Eva. Several taller people blocked her from view. But then they spotted her struggling with two suitcases, one filled with books and the other with clothes, the sum total of her possessions at Radcliffe.

Dr. Howard rushed forward. "Hello, Dr. Dykes," he greeted her, smiling. When she spied her favorite uncle Eva dropped the suitcases and embraced him.

"Hello, Doctor. Hello, Pum Pum." James Dykes, Eva's father, had left the family while Eva was still quite young. Her mother, Martha, had later married a Mr. Pumphrey. The children called her "Pum Pum" or "Pumpie."

Anita ran forward and hugged her older sister. "We're so proud of you." Stepping back, she looked long at Eva. "I want to see if all that learning has made you grow any." They all laughed as they took her suitcases.

When they arrived home and sat in comfortable chairs, they started prying her with questions.

"Where's your dissertation?" Quickly Eva opened the largest suitcase and took out a big volume.

"Looks like an Oxford dictionary," Anita quipped. The 644-page hardbound dissertation was every bit of two-and-a-half inches thick. (The volume is now on file in the archives of the Eva B. Dykes Library at Oakwood College; a photocopy is in the Harvard Archives, Pusey Library.)

"I've never seen a dissertation that thick," Martha Ann commented. Eva loved the challenge of doing her very best at all times and had worked on her dissertation until she had exhausted the subject.

"I wrote on Pope. See, the title is 'Alexander Pope's Influence in America from 1810 to 1850'! I discovered, by chance, that he was very interested and sympathetic toward black people." Dr. Howard knew its contents well, for he had spent several hours reviewing her in preparation for her three-hour oral defense, the last requirement for her Doctor of Philosophy, which she completed March 21, 1921.

Having completed her requirements in March, Eva Dykes had been the first black woman in the United

States to earn a Ph.D., but she was not the first to receive her degree. Two had graduated the week before Eva: Georgianna R. Simpson, Ph.D. in German, from the University of Chicago on June 14; and Sadie Tanner Mozel, Ph.D. in economics, from the University of Pennsylvania on June 15. (The latter is now a retired lawyer and married Mr. Alexander, a Federal judge.) By a quirk of commencement scheduling, the first became last.

By now some friends had arrived, and Dr. Howard, still fondling the heavy dissertation volume, prepared to let them know of Eva's accomplishments.

Heredity and Heroes

The nation's capital experiences great periods of growth during times of crisis. Large numbers of people move to Washington, D.C., to handle jobs resulting from the Federal Government's efforts to meet such emergencies.

During the Civil War the Howards worked as slaves on a large estate in Howard County, Maryland. Now free and in need of jobs, they joined the thousands migrating to the nation's capital to look for work in the aftermath of the Civil War. The city's population soared from 60,000 to 120,000. In addition to employment, many freedmen wanted their children to have the best educational advantages. Such was the case with John and Rebecca Howard and their four children.

All four Howard children enrolled in Howard University's Preparatory School. Floda Howard graduated with honors in 1888, stayed around Washington for a while, then moved west to Oklahoma. Eva says she never knew her uncle Floda, since he had died before her birth. John Howard, Jr., after finishing at the Preparatory School, attended the College of Arts and Science. When he received his B.A. with honors, he also went to Oklahoma to become a teacher, and Eva did not see him often. James

Howard graduated from the Preparatory School in 1876. Intrigued by higher education, he, too, enrolled in the college to work on his Bachelor's degree. Their only sister, Martha Ann, attended Howard, but because of illness had to withdraw. These last two, James Howard and Martha Ann Howard, would have a profound influence on Eva Dykes.

Attending the Howard University Preparatory School at about the same time as Martha Ann and James Howard was another brilliant young man named James Stanley Dykes. When he received his certificate in 1883 he entered the college and received his Bachelor of Arts in 1887, an honor graduate. Many students would come to him for tutoring in both math and Greek while he went to Howard and for many years after he graduated. Years later he remembered the subjects as vividly as if he had just graduated from college.

It was inevitable that Martha Ann Howard should meet and marry him. On Sunday, August 13, 1893, Eva Beatrice Dykes was born to them. (In that same month and year, two devout Methodist parents in Florida had a baby boy, Frank Loris Peterson. He would become an influential Black Adventist leader and would work with Eva.) The second child in the family of three girls, Eva was preceded by Florence (nicknamed Flossie) and followed by Anita. The Dykeses also had a son, but he died a few days after birth.

Heredity and environment were preparing Eva for a love of academia. Besides her parents and uncles, she had cousins and other relatives who were college-trained teachers and other professionals in Maryland and the District of Columbia.

Thirty years from slavery, and the Howards and

the Dykeses had already made a mark in the academic world. The greater percentage of black people in the nation and its capital were still illiterate, yet Eva would be exposed to Latin, Greek, French, music, math, literature, and Bible in her home. She would be a second-generation college graduate.

While Eva was quite young, James Dykes deserted the family and left his wife to raise the girls. Martha Ann felt a sense of uselessness and frustration. She had three small children, no husband, no job, no college degree, and was in ill health. How could she do it all?

Dr. Howard understood her distress. "Martha Ann, are you worried? Don't fret. God will provide. He always looks after His children. One parent completely dedicated can, with the help of God, do a sufficient job. The quality of the parenting is what's important. Let's pray about it."

Tears rushed to her eyes as she heard her brother pour out his heart to God on her behalf and for her children. She knew she could do it now. After the prayer he said, "Come live with me, Martha Ann. I have a big house. I'll arrange it with my wife. There's plenty of room, and there's plenty of love."

Martha Ann threw herself on the mercy of her brother and of God. At last she dared to hope that He would not only strengthen her frail body but would give her all the necessary maternal qualities to rear her children in the fear and admonition of the Lord. She had committed her case to the Lord, and He would provide.

Martha Ann devoted her entire life to preparing her daughters for the responsibilities she knew God would place on them in the future. Although she knew she would be criticized, she maintained her faith and her faithfulness. When other women visited at social gatherings, Martha Ann spent her time and energies caring for and teaching her children. She shared with their expanding minds her own piety and trust in Divine Providence. And her prayers and early training proved sufficient to sustain their relationship to God for the rest of their lives.

To an outsider their home seemed to be divided because the father had gone. But Martha Ann had pledged herself to her children, and Dr. Howard's affection and cooperation steadily supported her. In reality, it was a house of united love.

Before leaving home, the family would worship God early each morning. Often Martha prayed that He would strengthen her sickly body so that she could help her children complete their education.

Martha taught the girls to read while they were still in their petticoats. Every day she read to them from the Bible and had them read aloud the more interesting stories. Also she read them poetry and other literature.

Eva developed a passion for reading all sorts of books. While reading a little literature book, Eva became acquainted with Phillis Wheatley, who became her special heroine. She enjoyed learning about the frightened little slave girl brought to Boston by John Wheatley as a servant for his wife. The Wheatley children taught Phillis to read both English and Latin. At about 13 she began to write poetry. Years later she composed and sent one to President George Washington, who wrote back and thanked her for her "elegant lines." Phillis Wheatley gave Eva a greater appreciation for English, Latin, and literature, and a determination to help others understand the beauty of literature.

But foremost among Eva's heroes stood her uncle James—dignified, cultured, respected, learned, Christian, enthusiastic. Often when Dr. Howard came home in the evenings, his pockets bulged with presents for his nieces. After graduating from medical school, he practiced as a physician and at the same time served as a clerk in the U.S. War Department in Washington, D.C. Finally he gave up his practice and devoted all of his time to his government job.

Knowing of Eva's great interest in Phillis Wheatley, Dr. Howard later left the United States for Africa. While in Abyssinia he built a school for the education of Ethiopian girls.

James Howard made arrangements for Florence and Eva to study at the Berlitz French School. Dr. Dykes says that the instruction was private. "They didn't take colored people then. My uncle sent word that he had some nieces whom he wanted to enroll. They said, 'All right,' and agreed to give us lessons privately.

"They never spoke any English. When the tutors would come, they would only speak in French, and we didn't know what they were saying at first. We just repeated it. I thought they couldn't speak English. But we learned French very quickly. I continued after my sister Flossie became sick."

Dr. Howard saw that his nieces had an interest in music, so he arranged to buy a piano. They received lessons from the best instructors in Washington, D.C.

Later Martha Ann married Mr. Pumphrey, and the girls began to call their mother "Pum Pum." Mr. Pumphrey, a contractor, had little formal education and was quiet and unassuming. From time to time their father, now the principal of a school in Hagerstown, Maryland, would return to take the girls out riding. Always admiring the intellectual alertness of her father and his belief in hard work, Eva enjoyed his infrequent visits. And with the ever-present Dr. Howard about, the girls never felt the lack of a father figure in the home.

Martha Ann Dykes was a quiet, gentle mother, but a strict disciplinarian. "Spankings, yes, I was no exception," Eva recalls. "Our mother used to administer the gentle art of applying the hand or rod to the skin with such an effect that at the time of administering the punishment the recipient determined never to do anything that would cause the process to be repeated. But the passing of time erased all such resolutions from the childish mind."

She remembers her mother teaching her with relentless persistence. "Eva, whatever job you undertake, do it right and do your best." And Eva affirmed later that the satisfaction of doing her best brought a greater reward than the actual accomplishment of her aim.

Often her uncle used to repeat, "Never pay much attention to unprincipled things that might be said about you; only see that they will not be founded upon fact." He constantly reiterated a second principle, "Don't procrastinate, do it now, don't procrastinate."

Eva first went to the Teacher Training School at Howard University as a first-grade pupil, and stayed there until the fourth grade. It was the practice ground for students of Howard University's Teachers' College. She admired the young education students who could so easily explain the principles of Latin, Greek, English, and literature.

Dr. Dykes remembers that the other students

used to laugh at her at first because of her size. She was smaller than most of the other students, but they soon changed their opinion when they noticed that she accepted any challenge, no matter how big it might be, and that her work was always the very best. When they realized that she surpassed everyone in every subject she took, they decided that 13 must not be so bad after all.

When she would come home from school on Friday, she would practice her hymns in preparation for the church services she would accompany for on Sunday. Even at the age of 7 she was sought after in many churches in the Washington, D.C., area. During the rest of the week she arose at six o'clock to practice Bach, Beethoven, and Brahms.

She played for several Baptist and Methodist churches and early began to organize choirs. At 7 she played the organ for a Baptist church in Washington. "Because of my size," she says, "I could not use the pedal and the bellows at the same time. On one occasion when the members were having a social, my mother said I suddenly stopped playing, jumped down from the platform, and started marching. Everyone laughed at my joining in to march with the grown-ups."

She vividly remembers her third-grade teacher. Miss Barker, kind and sympathetic, loved nature. On one of their excursions into the park during a recess period they found a little dead bird. The woman sadly told the children, "Let's give him a funeral." With all the dignity, solemnity, and pomp that they could muster, they made a little grave for the bird, and with tears in their eyes, buried it. It was probably from her that Eva learned to open her heart to the beauty of nature and its creatures.

Leaving Howard Teacher Training School, she went to the Lucretia Mott Elementary School. It was a black institution named after a white nineteenth-century crusader for abolition and women's rights. On the wall of the school hung a picture of Mrs. Mott, with a description of her activities as a member of various antislavery societies, and her founding of the Society for Women's Rights in 1848. At an early age Eva recognized her membership in these two minorities—blacks and women—and she had a desire to help others like herself.

Finishing elementary school, she attended M Street High School, later renamed in honor of the poet Paul Laurence Dunbar. M Street High was considered one of the best black schools in the entire nation. The first strictly academic high school for blacks, it had a carefully selected faculty and student body. A high percentage of its students became medical doctors, doctors of philosophy, teachers, and other professionals.

Eva took the college preparatory courses. Dr. E. Smith, of Washington, D.C., a former classmate of Howard days, remembers that when others had to study hard, Eva grasped the material quickly. She put herself enthusiastically into her work and enjoyed every class she took, although English and literature especially thrilled her. She remembered the admonition of her mother, "Eva, do your best."

Her family practiced its religion. Every evening their frail mother closed the day with a devotional and a reading from the Bible and some appropriate portion of literature. Although Mr. Pumphrey and Pum Pum were good Methodists, Dr. Howard was a faithful member of the First Seventh-day Adventist church in Washington, D.C. Eva says, "When I was a mere child he took me to the First church in his arms. Although I believed in my head that Seventh-day Adventism was correct, I didn't believe it in my heart. I remember, at our daily worship periods, my uncle praying, 'Lord, remember Thy handmaidens, Flossie, Eva, and Anita. Help them to do their best. Help them to be diligent. Help them to face the big challenges of life. Remember Thy handmaidens.'

"As a result, I can sympathize with many people who linger a bit before joining the Adventist Church," Eva comments, "even though they know that it is the truth. To break with friends, customs, and habits to join the Seventh-day Adventist Church is difficult, a big sacrifice." As Dr. Dykes looks back over 90 years of life, her two biggest heroes remain her mother and her uncle. They were severe when necessary, but gentle even in their severity. And they were always willing to teach a lesson, always willing to help and improve.

Gwendolyn M. Ward, in a paper prepared for a sociology class, interviewed Dr. Dykes and asked her, "What was your greatest thrill?"

Dr. Dykes confided that perhaps her greatest was the last words spoken by her mother on her deathbed in East Hall at Oakwood College in 1945: "Eva, you've been a good daughter to me." Then Mrs. Pumphrey slipped into a coma and never regained consciousness. For Eva to know that she had lived up to the expectations of her greatest heroine was a great joy.

Dr. Howard passed away in 1936. But the two had indelibly stamped her character. From her mother and uncle, Eva learned tolerance, dignity, gentleness, perseverance, thoroughness, faithfulness, the value of work, consideration for the feelings of others, and the other qualities that characterized her entire life.

Summa Cum Laude

In 1866 members of the First Congregational Society proposed setting up a school for the 4 million Negroes freed at the end of the Civil War. They decided to name it for General Oliver Otis Howard, who headed the postwar Freedmen's Bureau. He held a deep and revolutionary belief that former slaves could be educated, and that the advantages of higher education should be made available to all regardless of race, sex, creed, or national origin. The university was chartered and opened in 1867. Little did its founders know the profound influence the institution of learning would have on the black population of the United States.

At first it was only a theological seminary for black ministers. Shortly after, it expanded to include the training of teachers and shortened its name from "The Howard Normal and Theological Institute for the Education of Teachers and Preachers" to "Howard University."

The fledgling university initially had its headquarters in a three-story red-frame building near the present site of Howard University Hospital. In June, 1867, the institution purchased a 149-acre tract and as the finances of the Freedmen's Bureau permitted, erected new buildings. Over the next six decades

Howard University developed slowly but steadily, training scores of the nation's black professionals in a wide range of fields. Before 1926, however, Howard University in many ways was a university in name only. Its limited resources—though not the dedication of its teachers—confined it to second-class status in the world of American higher education.

In 1910, after graduating with distinction from M Street High School, Eva entered Howard University. When she enrolled, President Wilbur D. Thirkield, its ninth president, was a great advocate of industrial and vocational education, as was his successor Stephen M. Newman, president of Howard when Eva graduated. Many blacks found themselves caught up in the controversy over which should have priority: the training of the head or that of the hand.

The famous Booker T. Washington, of Tuskegee Institute, won many supporters by advocating industrial education as the only approach. Dr. W. E. B. DuBois, on the other hand, opposed this philosophy, and there still lingered some contention about the philosophy of black education when Eva enrolled at Howard. To her, the development of her mind must come first.

She had large doses of Latin, Greek, German, English literature, English language, and history. Her program included one unit each of trigonometry, botany, geology, and psychology; she took a total of twenty-four units in four years to complete her requirements for the B.A. degree. But of all her subjects she loved literature and language the most. Eva breezed through her course work and graduated from the College of Liberal Arts in 1914—the first student up to that time who had ever graduated with highest honors. The daughter of a Latin and Greek scholar who passed the love of languages on to his children, she appropriately received a B.A. degree with the Latin phrase "summa cum laude."

She had made an arrangement to teach at Walden University. But at her uncle's suggestion, after one year she applied for admission to Radcliffe in 1915. He signed the application blank for her admission, and made the financial arrangements.

Eva was somewhat disappointed that Radcliffe did not accept her for the Master's program. In spite of her excellent record, they were willing to accept her only as an unclassified student.

Lela M. Gooding, in her report on Dr. Dykes, states, "Radcliffe's posture was understandable. A prestigious Ivy League institution, its standards were known to be higher than average, and jealous of its reputation, it was not about to accept another college's graduate into its graduate program without a trial period. Besides, students of black institutions were singularly suspect: Howard University, like other black schools, had in the old days repeatedly lowered its requirements to accommodate the new freedmen, and old reputations die hard.

"From Radcliffe's point of view, Eva Dykes' summa cum laude was not particularly impressive. Another reason for her 'unclassified' status, was the fact that, other things being equal, by Radcliffe's standards Eva's degree in liberal arts did not include enough units of English to qualify her for the Master's program. Howard University's curriculum had called for as many units of Latin, Greek, and German as of English.

"Undiscouraged and undaunted, Miss Dykes plunged into her studies. Her years as an unclassified student consisted of a full program of English, along with one Latin class, and she made honor grades in each. At the end of the year, Dr. Howard received notification from Radcliffe that his niece would be qualified for a B.A. degree after another year.

"So there was more English, a little French and Latin, and at the end of the year a second B.A. degree. There were 105 young ladies in that graduating class. One of them graduated summa cum laude, and Eva was one of the thirteen in the next-highest honor level, magna cum laude (with high distinction). She graduated in the top 13 percent of her class, perhaps even higher, for her Radcliffe undergraduate transcript, except for two 'B's,' which were also honor grades (so noted on the official transcripts of students of Radcliffe), showed all 'A's.'

"In moving on to Radcliffe, Eva had dared what no other member of her family had dared or cared to do: she had assailed the white academic world. And her performance in the undergraduate level indicated that she was equipped to compete on their level as an equal—in fact, as one of their best."

When she graduated from Howard as the valedictorian of her class, she won the Alpha Kappa Alpha (America's first black sorority, founded at Howard in 1908) Scholastic Award for excellence in scholarship. It consisted of only $10. Now Radcliffe, the institution that had trouble accepting her, also decided to award her a scholarship. Each year, after her first year, she received several hundred dollars, which during the early 1900s was a considerable sum. Whatever else she needed her uncle supplied. Her undergraduate work at Radcliffe was of such high caliber that she was elected to Phi Beta Kappa, a society reserved for the most scholarly university students. While she worked on her B.A., a news item appeared in the

January 14, 1917, Washington, D.C., *Sunday Star.* "Word has been received from Boston that two young Washington women had won honor grades at Radcliffe College. Miss Elizabeth Brandeis, daughter of a Justice of the Supreme Court, is one of the fine juniors to rank with 'very high academic distinction,' and Miss Eva B. Dykes is one of the seniors who has ranked with 'marked excellence.'"

Two significant events happened while Eva attended Radcliffe, one tragic and one joyful. September classes were in full swing when she received a telegram from Washington. "Flossie very sick, come home," it urged.

The house seemed somber, even though the sun shone brightly when Eva entered. She had managed to skip her Friday class so that she could spend the weekend with Flossie. Her sister had never looked more beautiful to Eva—young, intelligent, with brooding eyes, sensitive mouth, and neatly braided hair bound about her head. But Flossie's slender frame lay twisted in pain under the covers.

"How are you, Flossie?"

The girl couldn't answer audibly, but her pain-stricken eyes gave her reply. Eva's heart missed a beat. "Pum Pum, she's really sick. Where's Doctor?"

"He and several other doctors were just here. He's gone to church. Friday his pocket league meets." Dr. Howard had organized the King's Pocket League, which distributed hundreds of tracts, brochures, and booklets every week.

"She's worsened since he left."

"I'll go get him." It was night when she returned.

The grief-stricken faces around the bed watched in silence. Tears slipped from Martha Ann's eyes. Eva's face mirrored unbelief and shock.

On October 5, 1917, her closest sister, Flossie, died suddenly and mysteriously. Flossie had also been an honor graduate of Howard, and had taught in the commercial college of Howard University (a department of the university discontinued in 1919). The girl was young, talented, and gifted. She, like her sister, was interested in music and literature and had been teaching French and music. Dr. Howard would have sent her to Radcliffe also if she had lived. Her death was a bitter experience for the entire family, but especially for Eva. Death can be a blessed release for those in pain and suffering. But when it suddenly strikes one in the prime of life, it is a shock difficult to accept.

Martha Ann and Eva brooded over the tragedy. Often what seems a tragedy can be a pathway to a deeper experience. The Holy Spirit made an appeal to their hearts in their evening worships. Dr. Howard talked more pointedly about the state of the dead, explaining what had really happened to Flossie, and slipped in other beliefs of Seventh-day Adventists.

This experience made Eva more concerned about her own health. Many friends claimed that Flossie had died of cancer of the stomach, and Eva was always concerned, even afraid, that she might be a later victim. Adventism, with its emphasis on health, seemed more appealing than ever before.

The second event would determine the direction of her life more than she ever realized. Early in Eva's life her mother had become a member of the Ashbury Methodist church. Dr. Howard had continued to witness quietly and explain the Sabbath teaching, but to no avail. But while Eva was at Radcliffe a fiery new minister came to the Ephesus church. Although he was there only from 1916 to 1923, the congregation grew from forty to almost three hundred under his leadership. Elder P. Gustavus Rodgers would visit the homes of the members, and if he saw a need he would see that it was supplied. A true pastor and a powerful evangelist, he never relaxed his efforts in teaching his candidates the necessity of following God's commandments.

Dr. Howard influenced his sister to visit Elder Rodgers' tent effort. The truth was so powerful that she returned night after night. She received Bible studies and was eventually baptized.

Now that both her uncle and her mother were members of the Adventist Church, Eva felt she must investigate its teachings. What she had formerly known in her mind now became a reality in her heart.

The year he baptized Martha Ann, Elder Rodgers had another tent meeting on Sherman Avenue and Irving Street NW., Washington, D.C. Eva was baptized on December 5, 1920, with twenty-eight candidates. Among them were Joseph and Willie Anna Dodson, who had given up their jobs to join the Adventist Church. The Dodsons would later become close friends of Eva and would play an important part in the formation of the denomination's regional conferences.

The Lord allowed Joseph Dodson to open his own taxicab business to compensate for the loss of his job, and later he became proprietor of the college store at 2610 Georgia Avenue. It sold books and other supplies to Howard University students. Willie Anna Dodson served as a highly respected principal at several Washington schools.

A High-class High School

Dunbar High School, formerly M Street High, was at the zenith of its golden age when Eva, now working on her dissertation at Radcliffe, accepted the offer to affiliate with its teaching staff.

When she successfully defended her dissertation (the school gave her a few days' leave to take her orals) and completed her requirements for her degree, she received a letter from her new boss:

"April 5, 1921

"Miss Eva Dykes
"Dunbar High School
"My dear Miss Dykes:

"I am writing to extend to you a most sincere congratulations upon your success in winning from Radcliffe College your Ph.D. Considered from any angle, this is a worthy accomplishment.

"No other colored woman in America has won yet such a distinction; and very few men of color have obtained such honors; in fact, few are the persons who enter the ranks of scholars.

"Very sincerely,
"Garnet C. Wilkinson, Principal
"Paul Laurence Dunbar High School"

When she reported back to work, Mr. Wilkinson met her at the door, quickly opened it for her, tipped his imaginary hat, bowed, and said, "Pleased to meet you, Dr. Eva B. Dykes."

"Dr. Eva B. Dykes." She had to get used to the sound of it—she would hear it often during the next nine years at Dunbar and for the rest of her life.

Dunbar attracted the black elite living in Washington. When a student left Dunbar, he had recognition in the academic world. The school had moved from M Street two blocks over and now was located on New Jersey Avenue at N Street. The first building had become old and outdated. But so many former students had such love and respect for M Street High that they returned to pick up bricks and pieces of the old building to carry home so they could always remember their beloved school. The founders had wanted to rebuild it in the same location, but insufficient space prevented them from developing the new plant on the same site. Now in a new spot, it also received a new name—Dunbar High.

Dr. Simpson, one of the other black women who had received her Ph.D. in 1921 with Eva Dykes, also came to Dunbar. The two pioneer female doctors taught side by side at the new institution. The other black Ph.D., Dr. Mozel, also worked in Washington. All three of the women had graduated from Washington, D.C., schools, and now they returned to contribute to their hometown.

Besides teaching, Dr. Dykes had responsibility for developing the school's social life. Helen Sugland, one of her students, and later a good friend, remembers her giving and directing plays at Dunbar. One of her plays was mostly in French, and Dr. Dykes's Berlitz training made her an excellent French teacher and stage director.

The Washington, D.C., *Evening Star* on Friday, March 19, 1926, mentioned the national oratorical contest that Dr. Dykes supervised. Under the title "Oratory Rivalry Keen at Dunbar," the *Star's* article stated that the contest was "of supreme value, not only to the contestants who shall have benefited immeasurably by their preparation, but also to the other students whose attention during the hearing of the oration will be focused upon the supreme law of the land, the Constitution." It then recognized Dr. Dykes's part in organizing and spearheading the program.

Mr. Walter Smith, an unusual homeroom teacher, gave meaningful daily guidance to the boys' section of Dunbar High. Later Mr. Smith became principal of Dunbar and had to rate Eva's teaching performance. One's peers are sometimes the most critical and judgmental. On the several yearly teacher rating sheets that still exist, he rated her as VG (very good) and ES (eminently superior).

To be an eminently superior teacher at an eminently superior school, dealing with eminently superior students, under an eminently superior principal, was a difficult job, but one that Dr. Dykes fulfilled.

Dr. Dykes taught invaluable lessons to the adolescents that sat in her classroom. Lessons of English and Latin, yes, but also lessons of character and quality. She treated each student as an individual, and was thoroughly dedicated to her work. Concerned about the total student, she was interested to see that they would cultivate the social graces that would help them to be leaders in their society and in their circle of friends. Most felt that she worked beyond the call of duty, and looked up to her as a perfectionist in all that she did.

When Eva began teaching at Dunbar in September of 1920, she was not an Adventist, but the Spirit of God was tugging at her heart. Once she was baptized in December and had finally made the surrender to the Holy Spirit, she let everyone know that she was an Adventist.

Previously she had not seen the importance of observing the seventh-day Sabbath, but now that it was clear to her, she determined that she would follow it all the way, come what may. Many of her colleagues ridiculed her, and some suggested that too much learning had made her mad.

Eva continued with persistence and with outstanding service, and soon her faith and her brilliant example had its rewards. "Do you really believe this doctrine?" they asked.

"Certainly I do, or I would not live it," she answered without hesitation. "I lay myself, my talent, my reputation, my all upon the altar of God. It is my duty to help Him to the extent of my power, to witness every day, in whatever way I can."

Although Dr. Dykes chaired many functions, Mr. Walter Smith's faculty soon learned that she would not take part in any school function on Friday night or during the rest of the Sabbath. To accommodate her, the administration changed the regular Saturday morning colloquium to Friday morning, and readily gave permission for her to meet with parents at other times besides the Friday night teachers' meetings.

Her cousin Agnes Dykes, whose parents had died when she was small, came to live with Eva while she taught at Dunbar. Agnes was some 12 or 13 years younger. Eva had just joined the church and was most eager to impress her younger cousin with Adventism. Carefully she explained how Adventists didn't go to the movies and didn't drink, and all of the other beliefs that the church considered important. "Well, she convinced me," the cousin admitted, "but I hadn't given my life to Christ, so I continued living as before.

"Even though Eva was older than I was, we were about the same size, and I used to wear her clothes. I would come in late at night from the movies, dressed in Eva's clothes, and I would joke with my cousin and say, 'Eva, you may not have been to the movies, but your clothes went last night. This dress sat in a theater seat and these shoes have walked where sinners have trod.' I used to laugh and kid her, but she continued to witness in a very quiet way. Even though today I am a Catholic, I consider myself a 'Seventh-day Adventist Catholic,' and am still asking that the Lord will help me accept the truth."

Eva laughs when she recalls one of her little nieces who couldn't say Aunt Eva, but used to say "Aunt Evil." Distinctly she remembers the girl praying, ". . . and deliver us from evil," and then opening one eye and looking up at "Aunt Evil."

Dr. Dykes was a strict disciplinarian. Whenever she played the piano for Dunbar's enormous student body, it was absolutely necessary that one could hear a pin drop before she would touch the piano. One bright young boy, Nathaniel, use to stomp into her classroom. He had received education at West Point and no doubt still envisioned himself as a soldier. She had him stay after school and practice coming in again and again until his feet could manuever his body quietly to his designated seat.

Nathaniel was attracted to this young teacher who

took a real interest in his personal development, and on many occasions he sought her out for special counsel. Even after he graduated, he continued his relationship with Dr. Dykes. On one occasion she slipped him some material that explained the Sabbath. Later he returned and said, "I am very much impressed with the tracts you have been giving me, but there is only one problem. It would be wonderful if there were people today who were keeping God's day."

Eva replied, "There are people who keep God's day." Through her influence he became an Adventist, married a staunch Seventh-day Adventist, Lillian Burgess, and went on to Oakwood.

Nathaniel Ashby later became an outstanding teacher, principal of Washington Union Academy (Dupont Park), and minister of the Adventist Church. Ashby Auditorium at Oakwood College stands as a memorial not only to him but also to Dr. Dykes, the teacher who insisted that he do his best and do it right.

She not only counseled those who needed help, but also inspired the talented group of students who sat under her. A high percentage of her students left to become medical doctors, doctors of philosophy, professors, government employees, and eminently superior citizens.

Many later made outstanding contributions to this country. Charles Drew did pioneer research in blood plasma preservation and was responsible for the blood banks that saved countless lives of soldiers and civilians during World War II. William Hastie became dean of Howard University Law School and then was appointed governor of the Virgin Islands in 1946. President Truman asked him to serve on the U.S. Court of Appeals in 1949. Joseph Jenkins served as an outstanding English professor at Tuskegee Institute. Many of those who have made outstanding contributions to the church and society drew inspiration from this diminutive woman.

It was her goal not only to give of her best to the Master, but also to see that each student gave of his best and reached his highest potential.

Students sometimes forgot the rules of grammar that she drilled into them, but they couldn't forget her. She was unforgettable. Marguerite Chin Robinson expresses the impression she made on her students.

"September 1, 1977

"Dear Dr. Dykes:

"My assignment is to get out the invitations to the faculty members, and I simply cannot resist inserting this personal note. You were my English teacher for three semesters at Dunbar, and you were the best! I remember so vividly the courses and your dedication to the growth of each student.

"You are a far distance away, but if you could manage to get here for this fiftieth anniversary, you would make us quite happy and oh, so proud!

"You had so many students that it's highly probable that you won't remember me, but I shall never, never forget you."

School in Washington

Today more than a score of Adventist churches dot the Greater Washington, D.C., area. In the late 1800s one lone church, First church, witnessed for the Adventist faith in the nation's capital. First church's congregation was interracial, the blacks outnumbering the whites three to one. Like Onesimus and Philemon, former slaves and former masters worshiped there as brothers and friends in Christ.

Adventist believers had appeared in Washington, D.C., as early as 1876, but no permanent presence existed for some time. Various individuals labored to develop an interest, until a city mission was set up at 1831 Vermont Avenue NW. A church was officially organized February 24, 1889, with twenty-six charter members, including Dr. James Howard.

A row house with a double parlor served as lecture room and provided living quarters for a staff that numbered as many as seven. They sold books and periodicals from door to door to cover expenses and then followed up their sales with visits, Bible studies, and invitations to their Sabbath meetings.

The mission moved from Vermont Avenue to a southeast site near the United States Capitol. In 1893 the group purchased a small church building on

Eighth Street NE., between F and G streets. Among its members was Mrs. Rosetta Douglass Sprague, daughter of Frederick Douglass.

Among the speakers in First church was Mrs. Ellen G. White. At this time the General Conference still had its headquarters in Battle Creek, Michigan.

Several evangelists, both black and white, came to conduct meetings in Washington. Because some of the leaders were concerned with the difficulty of reaching the white population in a segregated city, they advised the establishment of separate congregations, and the Second Adventist church of Washington organized with about forty members in September, 1902.

Most of the whites left First church to attend the new congregation. Its building had been purchased from contributions solicited in the *Review and Herald* and was called Memorial church, since now Adventism had an adequate "memorial for God" in the capital from which contacts could be made with men of influence.

Later another little group of black believers, twenty-five worshipers, met in various homes around Northwest Washington, finally settling in the home of Mrs. David Jones. One Sabbath, Elder R. E. Harter, the president of the District of Columbia Conference, met with the little company. At the close of his Spirit-filled sermon, the people took a vote, and a second black church, later to become Dupont Park church, came to life.

The conference officials unbelievably decided to purchase a church building for the members. Together with the Columbia Union, they purchased a structure in 1916 and gave it outright to the struggling group of believers. A committee selected the name "Ephesus," the same name of the early Christian church that means "first" or "desirable." Since there was already a First church, Ephesus for them meant "desirable."

The Ephesus church voted to accept the building that the German Reformed church was selling on the corners of Sixth and N streets NW. Now that it was an · organized church with a building, their first full-time minister arrived in the person of Elder Ulysses S. Willis, Sr. (His son, Elder Robert Willis, has also pastored it.)

The twenty-five members rattled in the large and spacious church. Elder Willis remained at Ephesus less than a year, and toward the end of 1916, Elder P. G. Rodgers arrived. It was he who baptized Martha Ann Pumphrey and Eva Dykes. (He was followed by R. L. Bradford, father of Charles Bradford; J. B. Mallory; E. C. Atkinson; J. G. Dasent; Joseph Dodson, a layman, who served as pastor in an interim period; J. E. Johnson; J. H. Wagner; T. M. Fountain; and W. Albert Thompson.)

While Ephesus church slowly grew, First church, on the other side of town, was also developing. Certain statements by Ellen White troubled the members of the two black Adventist churches in Washington. One admonished, "Gather your children into your own houses; gather them away from those who are disregarding the commandments of God, who are teaching and practicing evil. . . . Establish church schools. Give your children the word of God as the foundation of all their education."—*Testimonies*, vol. 6, p. 195.

The first church school in Washington, D.C., was held in 1916 in the home of Mrs. David Jones. Mrs. Inez Budd, Mrs. Alice Brown, and Mrs. Freeland served as the charter teachers. After the purchase of the Ephesus church at Sixth and N streets, the school occupied one small room at the rear of the prayer meeting room. Soon the school added another small room.

As it continued to expand, it was necessary to provide for more classrooms. The church decided to divide the lecture room in the basement into three classrooms and a chapel and secured more desks and seats.

Meanwhile on the other side of town a regular business meeting of the First church, October 13, 1920, appointed a ways and means committee to study a plan for organizing their own school. At this time several of the First church children were attending the classes already started at the Ephesus church.

Only twenty-three church members pledged their support of a school that would hold twelve children at First church. Since it was not large enough a support to foster such a great undertaking, the church disbanded the committee and dropped the matter.

The Spirit of the Lord continued to work upon the hearts of the people, and they made many feeble efforts to start a school. Finally, after much discussion and great opposition, classes began in the basement of First church.

These first church schools, located in the basement and back rooms of the two churches, were the seeds for the Adventist education system in Washington, D.C. The zealous leadership of Elder P. G. Rodgers, assisted by the loyal teachers, resulted in an increased enrollment.

The school year of 1925-1926 marked the merging of the two church schools at the Ephesus church, under the name of Washington Union Academy. First church closed its basement facilities. Many parents who had opposed the church school now began to look upon it with favor.

The financing of the school had always been a problem, and the merging increased the difficulty. The janitorial service, heating, teachers' salaries, and equipment were difficult problems.

September, 1926, opened with an enrollment of thirty-five pupils. The following year saw fifty pupils. The year 1928-1929 was the last year that the Washington Union Academy conducted classes at the Ephesus church. The question of the appropriateness of the Ephesus basement as the place for the school became an issue in the business meetings of both churches.

In 1923, Dr. James Howard's wife had died, and to take his mind off the tragedy, he had gone to Abyssinia. While there he became interested in building an Adventist school for the education of Ethiopian girls. Meeting Emperor Haile Selassie, he collaborated with him in the school project. Shortly before he left the United States, Eva's uncle gave her power of attorney in all of his affairs and turned his house over to her. Because he knew how difficult it would be for his family, he left without informing anyone of his departure. The family was concerned about his whereabouts until they received a letter stating that he was in Africa fulfilling a lifelong dream.

He named the school after his dead wife, Isabella Marion Cook. Having been married to him since 1886, she was the mother of the famous composer Will Marion Cook and grandmother of Mercer Cook, a teacher of Romance languages in Washington.

When he returned to Washington a year later, he reentered government service, and in 1925 married an affluent kindergarten teacher, Miss Retha Dillard.

Now that his nieces were grown he didn't have to be with them to guide them as before. Flossie had died, Anita had gotten married, and Eva was now teaching at Dunbar. He moved into a new house with his new wife. Dr. Howard now determined that the black Adventist youth of Washington would have an adequate school, and he plunged all of his ability into its development.

With a heavy burden he left First church after one special meeting and headed slowly toward the home of his sister and niece. The cause of Christian education for black boys and girls in the capital city seemed doomed.

The faith of the members was small, and funds were insufficient. No one seemed willing to contribute the necessary sum that would allow them to move the school out of the basement. As he walked along, the burden pressed on him.

He knew that he owed on the house that he and his wife had just moved into. But the one that he had just given to Eva was debt-free. Now he prayed that his niece would go along with the idea to let him place a large mortgage on that house to obtain money to build the new school.

Solemnly he called Martha Ann and Eva into the room and explained to them his idea. Eva didn't hesitate. "Doctor," she said, "I agree with you, for we must provide a school for our young people here in Washington. Let's go to the bank tomorrow and arrange for a loan."

In 1929, a $6,000 mortgage on a home was a great deal of money. But without any hesitation, Eva agreed to have one placed on her home. After the bank had agreed that the house at 1724 Eighth Street would act as collateral for the money, Dr. Howard had to convince the members of First church to participate in the repayment of the loan.

A convincing speaker, he showed the need for Christian education and explained how he had just come back from Ethiopia, where he had set up a school. If education was necessary for black people in Africa, it was even more so for the American black Seventh-day Adventist.

During the month of April, 1929, Dr. Howard had some building materials placed in the basement of the First church, to be used with the consent of the church for the new school. On May 4, 1929, after several hours of discussion and prayer, First church voted to accept the loan of $6,000 and thirty-four members pledged to pay the monthly note. In August of the same year an additional loan of $2,000 enabled them to complete the building. By September the new building consisted of five classrooms of various sizes, with basement rooms.

Eva, having consented to let the mortgage be placed on her house, continued to be generous with the church school and with everything connected with it. The school was now located at 624 Eighth Street NE. The 1929 Washington Union Academy school year opened with an unprecedented enrollment of more than one hundred students.

When Elder Jacob Justiss became pastor of Ephesus church, he realized that the congregation had outgrown the old building and the Washington Union Academy. With the dream of a new and bigger structure, the church began to construct the new plant, which would finally cost $1 million. The indebtedness was such that it was important for the school to be as self-supportive as possible.

Elder J. L. Moran, who had been president of Oakwood College and one of the founders of Pine Forge Academy, had retired, and now the conference had persuaded him to come out of retirement to be the first principal in the new school building. The school, formerly the joint enterprise of First church and Ephesus, became the sole responsibility of the Ephesus church, and its name changed from Washington Union Academy to Dupont Park School. The church also adopted the name of Dupont Park church.

Dr. Owen Troy, Sr., Elder Walter Starks, and Elder William DeShay worked hard to pay off the loans. During Elder William DeShay's leadership Dupont Park completely liquidated its debt, and the members dedicated the church and the school to the Lord.

Whereas the first church building had been an outright gift from the union and the conference, this one had been paid for by hard work and sacrifice by the congregation. Today, Dupont Park church, formerly Ephesus, boasts a membership of more than one thousand. First church has a congregation of eight hundred.

The school had thrived under Elder Moran's direction, and continued to do so under the leadership of Principal Edward Mattox, until it literally outgrew itself.

Elder J. Milton Thomas, the next pastor, faced the problem of whether to add to the present structure, build a new one in another location, or to buy another building. On Alabama Avenue was a private school, but the price was prohibitive. Under the leadership of John C. Smith, however, negotiations for it began again, and the church purchased the property on Alabama Avenue for $321,000.

The three acres include not only the school itself but also two brick houses that face Alabama Avenue, a storage for Community Services, and a separate chapel.

With Elder John C. Smith as pastor of the Dupont Park SDA church, and Edward Mattox, Jr., as school administrator, operations began on two campuses in September, 1973, with grades kindergarten through six and the administrative offices housed in the Alabama Avenue building. Mr. Kenneth Palmer became the principal and Mrs. Margaret Williams the assistant principal, responsible for the building on Alabama Avenue.

The full list of the administrators of the school throughout its history are Mr. E. M. Lane, Mrs. Janette Anderson, Mrs. Elsie Gumbs, Mrs. Alma J. Scott, Miss Myrtle Gates, Miss Margaret Booker, Mr. Garland J. Millet, Mr. I. A. Christian, Mr. A. Wellington Clark, Mr. Nathaniel E. Ashby, Mrs. Fitzgerald Jenkins, Mr. Jacob Justiss, Mrs. Myrtle Gates Murphy, Mrs. Maggie Montgomery, Mrs. Mae E. Justiss, Elder James L. Moran, Mr. Edward Maddox, Jr., Mr. Kenneth Palmer, Mrs. Margaret Norman Williams, and Mr. William M. Mathi.

Literally hundreds of institutions of learning of all kinds, purposes, and sizes crowd the nation's capital. Washington is an educational center as well as a political hub. Inasmuch as it was the only Seventh-day Adventist school in the city of Washington, it was God's school, founded in the hope that its light would shine with ever-increasing intensity to and through all who would attend.

From its feeble beginnings in 1916, from the

church basements and back rooms, from Washington Union Academy, and now from Dupont Park School, hundreds of graduates have gone out to carry the message of the crucified, risen, and soon-coming Saviour to all the world.

It does not have the most spacious corridors or the largest playgrounds, but it climbs far above other schools in Washington because it teaches the divine attributes of the greatest Teacher of all ages, Jesus Christ.

The teachers, members, and the Home and School fellowships have contributed equipment and the moral support that have made the institution what it is today. They have taken seriously the statement "Churches where schools are established may well tremble as they see themselves entrusted with moral responsibilities too great for words to express."—*Testimonies*, vol. 6, p. 204.

This Christian institution still is the only Seventh-day Adventist school in the nation's capital.

SFTID-4

A Daughter of Howard

The polished mahogany doors to the president's office closed behind the visitor whom a secretary had just ushered in. The office appeared empty until the high-backed chair swiveled around and revealed a fair-skinned black man. "Come in! Come in!" the president beckoned.

"I understand that you requested to see me."

"Yes, that's right. I'd like to invite you to join the English faculty of Howard. I'm sure your work at Dunbar is satisfying, but we're trying to build up this department by adding four new teachers this year. I want to raise the total staff of the English Department to twelve, and we need three doctors instead of just the two we have now."

"You know this is my alma mater," Eva began.

"Sure, I know Dr. Howard and your family. I've studied your record. I know your accomplishments." Smiling suavely, he beckoned her to be seated. "That's why I sent for you."

The atmosphere became a little more relaxed as Dr. Johnson crossed his legs. He talked about the university and his dream of a strong academic institution. After about twenty minutes he stood up. "We have your records from Howard, of course. But we need your records from Radcliffe and a letter from

Dunbar. Send these to the dean."

"I'll see that they get to him along with a letter explaining my convictions."

"Your convictions?" His eyebrow raised.

"Yes. The letter will explain." The interview over, they shook hands, and he conducted her to the door.

Dr. Mordecai Wyatt Johnson, Howard University's thirteenth and first black president, elected to the office in 1926, had already gained recognition as a persevering worker for his people. A minister and powerful orator, he began to negotiate with the Federal Government for an annual appropriation. Wanting more than just better buildings, he dreamed of the most qualified staff available. Word of Dr. Dykes's amazing teaching abilities circulated in all of the Washington educational circles.

Some years later in an address before the students and faculty of the Seventh-day Adventist Theological Seminary, then located in Takoma Park, Washington, D.C., Mordecai Johnson explained the complications that her arrival caused and the surprise of that letter:

"I feel especially near to you in this church, too, because one of the finest teachers I have ever known came from your church. Her name is Dr. Eva B. Dykes. When I first came to Howard University, her name was brought to my attention in a peculiar way. She had received a Doctor's degree some time earlier from Radcliffe, and we were about to engage her as a teacher.

"Prior to taking the job, she had a conference with the dean, saying, 'Before you conclude this contract there is one thing you should know about me. I do not know if after you hear this you will wish to employ me or not, but I feel I must tell you I am a member of the

Seventh-day Adventist Church, and beginning at sundown on Friday until sundown Saturday I will be unable to do any work for the university, for in that period my church is foremost in my allegiance, and I shall feel under obligation to do whatever they wish me to do and will be able to give no service to the university.' The dean brought her letter to me (he was the first Negro in the United States to get his degree in Germany) and said, 'Mr. President, this is a very sad matter. I suppose this finishes it. We cannot employ this young woman. What a tragedy!' But I said to the dean, 'This does settle it. This makes certain we are going to employ this young woman.'

" 'What do you mean, Mr. President? We cannot hire someone who has reservations about service.'

"I replied, 'This is not a reservation but an affirmation. And I would further suggest that any woman who has the center of her life so dedicated is worth keeping, and we should not run the risk of losing a young person of that type. She will be just as loyal to the university the other six days as she is to her church on the Sabbath.' "

Dr. Johnson respected Dr. Dykes's religious convictions. He was a practicing Christian and an effective minister of the gospel. In 1930 Rabbi Stephen Wise chose him as one of the ten greatest religious leaders in the country. The Howard University president was determined to see her on his staff.

Dr. Dykes went on to reward the faith he had placed in her. She saw to it that she remained at the top of the profession. Taking and teaching summer classes, she joined and held memberships in many professional organizations and was as active in them as her schedule permitted. Also she was a member of and (when possible) chaired many college committees such as the student activities committee, the catalog committee, and the freshman committee. Even beyond that, she advised and sponsored various campus organizations. That she still found time to grade papers and make lesson plans testifies to her boundless energy.

Often Dr. Howard would drop by the university, looking for his niece, and not finding her in her teacher's cubbyhole correcting papers, he would search out his friend George William Cook, dean of the commercial school, and former dean of the Liberal Arts College. "Have you seen Eva?" he would call, and after exchanging greetings, the dean would indicate the last place that he had observed her.

George Cook called Eva a daughter of Howard University since so many of her family had passed through the institution and had distinguished themselves so highly. Florence had taught in Howard's Commercial Department. Now Eva had returned to be a teacher.

Dr. Dykes authored numerous articles in religious and other black journals, among them the *Crusader, The Negro History Bulletin, The Journal of Negro History, Message* magazine, the *Youth's Instructor*, and the *Review and Herald.* Her column, which still appears today in *Message,* began while she was at Howard in 1934. She edited and coedited the Howard University *Alumnus,* and authored several books.

Besides her writing, teaching, and school activities, she even had time on two occasions to do some "special work" in a private home.

She had a close friend at Ephesus church who worked for a prominent white family. Whenever extra guests came for dinner, the family would employ additional people.

Eva asked her friend Ada one day, "Next time Mrs. B needs extra help, can you suggest my name?"

"You're joking," Ada laughed.

"No, I'm not. I insist. I want the experience."

"OK," the friend agreed. "Buy a waitress' cap, a white apron, and a black uniform."

"Don't tell Mrs. B that I have a doctorate or that I teach at Howard University," Eva pleaded en route to the home.

When they arrived at their destination, Ada introduced her to Mrs. B. "I'm happy to meet you, Eva," the woman said. "Ada has told me that you have not worked as a waitress. I'll tell you what to do." She gave Dr. Dykes many points on how to hold the various dishes, how to serve the guests, and how to hold the champagne container. Then the woman concluded, "Eva, come to the parlor at six o'clock, stand at the door, and say, 'Madam, dinner is served.'"

As the guests entered, Eva had to stand behind each chair and hold it until each person was seated. Then she began serving the food. When she reached Mrs. B's chair, the hostess whispered, "Eva, you're doing fine." Dr. Dykes must have pleased her, for the woman requested her for another dinner party.

The apostle Paul said, "I am not ashamed of the gospel of Christ: for it is the power of God unto salvation." Once Eva had accepted Christ and the Seventh-day Adventist Church, she never apologized for or hid her beliefs.

One morning as she bounded up the steps and down the hall of the administration building, she met Mr. Anderson, a Howard University professor. "Good morning, Dr. Dykes. What's the good news for today?" he called out.

Without thinking, she replied, "Saturday is the seventh-day Sabbath. Why don't you keep it?"

Startled, he stood looking after her as she disappeared down the hall. Some time afterward he left Howard and became principal of a school in Coatesville, Pennsylvania. In later years Dr. Dykes attended a camp meeting, and to her surprise, encountered Mr. Anderson.

"Miss Dykes," he greeted, "do you know I am now a Seventh-day Adventist?"

"No," she said, her face expressing joy at the news.

"Yes," he continued. "Do you know that you are the one that started me thinking seriously about my spiritual condition? I became an Adventist in Coatesville after I had Bible studies with one of the old faithful members of the church. We have no church building as yet, but we hope to have one soon. I just want to say that those words you said one day in the hall at Howard made me think seriously of the Sabbath. Now I want to thank you for what you said to me that day."

Ephesus church was her life. It seemed to buoy her up and lift her spirits to face the week of teaching. Being the only Ph.D. in a large church was no problem to her. "Are you ever bored?" someone once asked her.

"No, I enjoy the company of the members of the church because there is a tie that binds members of the Seventh-day Adventist Church together all over the world," she replied.

Her friend Helen Sugland commented, "Dr. Dykes was someone, to paraphrase Rudyard Kipling, 'who could walk with the kings and queens and the higher-ups of the world, and yet not lose the common touch.'

"She would look around the church. If there were new members, she would invite them to dinner. Another time she might spot an elderly person and ask her home. She was not ashamed of the members of the family of God, none of them.

"Almost every week she had people over to her house and she was an excellent hostess. As superintendent of the Sabbath school she had wonderful programs. Nobody just got up and read the mission story. Knowing how to select the right people, she made them rehearse and practice until it was perfect.

"Dr. Dykes gave Bible studies everywhere. After teaching school all week she conducted them in various homes. She especially enjoyed Ingathering campaigns. Every Saturday evening she would organize a group who would stand at the corner of Seventh and P streets in Washington, where a bus stopped to let off passengers. As she would play the small organ for the singers, Mr. Montgomery, a teacher and father of Mrs. Alma Blackmon, would accompany her on his violin. People passing by would drop money into the can on the top of the portable organ.

"One evening Professor Syphax, of Howard University, got off the bus, and after congratulating them for their beautiful singing, dropped a dollar into the can. Another time Dr. Dykes saw another distinguished professor descend from the bus. He had not seen, or if he had, pretended not to have seen, his teaching colleague and began to cross the street. Quickly she left her organ and, marching quickly behind the professor, explained what she was doing. He placed a large donation in the can.

"She felt that the more important, the more learned, the richer you were, the more obligated you were to give a larger donation to the church and to

God's work."

Each year she would ask President Mordecai Johnson for a $50 or $100 donation (in those days a huge sum). Out of respect for his favorite teacher, he would always give.

Eva Dykes once commented about Dr. Mordecai Johnson, "He was interested in the comfort and welfare of his teachers and was never too busy to see his students and teachers. He said once that he had members 'ranging from agnostics, liberals, and fundamentalists, every denomination from Hindu to Seventh-day Adventist' serving on his faculty, which showed that he had a broad-minded attitude toward others. He himself was a Baptist minister, and he never publicly responded to any articles that appeared against him in the various news media."

The Dykes household had two pianos, one in the front living room, the other in the rear sitting room. Both of them seemed to get good use. Flossie usually played the one in the living room. She had a number of students who came to her house for piano lessons, and Eva would use the one in the rear. At six o'clock every morning you would find her seated at her bench. Such consistent practicing enabled her to be the accomplished pianist she was.

Eva always had an octet, a quintet, or a duet rehearsing with the piano. Many of those in her groups couldn't read notes, although they had a good ear, and she would pluck with one finger on the piano until they got it.

Her choirs were outstanding, and her groups received invitations to many churches. She loved to go places. Many times she and Helen Sugland would travel together.

In 1928 she managed to purchase her first car.

Helen Sugland tells the story like this: "I don't know who taught her to drive, but I remember the first time she bought a car, a little Ford. I rode in the car with her. She took the fenders off a white man's car. We were going out to Takoma Park, and he was just bringing his wife from the hospital, coming up Butternut Street to Georgia Avenue, when she turned too wide and ripped the fenders right off his car.

"Instantly she stopped, apologized, asked the possible cost of damages, and paid him right there." Her driving skills seemed to be her most glaring weakness. Through the years she worked on the problem and did become a good driver.

Although many thought her Ph.D would scare the bachelors away, she had many male admirers. But her faith in God's precepts was so profound that not even a marriage proposal changed her thinking.

According to Helen Sugland, she fell in love with Dr. Jasper Phillips, now deceased. "She was deeply in love with him, and he with her. They had met before she had joined the church, and had planned to get married, but after her baptism, she told him, 'I can't marry you unless you become a Seventh-day Adventist.' Then she explained the Sabbath and the other tenets of the Adventist Church.

"Dr. Phillips' father was a bishop in the Methodist Church, and he didn't want to leave his father's church. In spite of her affection for Phillips, the Holy Spirit led her not to marry out of the faith.

"He never married anyone else, and neither did she. As a matter of fact, years later, she wrote a song called 'The Ship That Never Comes In,' and he was the ship. One day she said to me, 'Helen, did you know that I wrote a song?' 'No, what kind of a song?' I replied. She said, 'Well, you know Dr. Phillips and I never got married, and my ship never came in, so I wrote "The Ship That Never Comes In." That's why I wrote it.'"

For fifteen years she played an aggressive role in the improvement of the several thousand black young people that sat in her classes. Sometime later she received the Howard University Alumni Award. In the citation Jason C. Grant, Jr., declared, "Few graduates of Howard University have led so rich and varied a life or one signalized by so many achievements as has Dr. Eva Beatrice Dykes." Then he went on to extol her academic, literary, and musical career.

He made special mention of her religious influence. "Even more prominent are her activities in the church. She is an untiring laborer in the church. The mere names of the positions she has held or holds in this institution attest not only to the broad range of her work there but also to the high confidence and esteem accorded her in this domain."

The final paragraph concluded, "Here, then, is a Howard graduate who has lived and is living a life not narrowed to the confines of a single category, but a full life characterized by a wide range of important activities and distinguished achievements. Such a life is in keeping with the highest humanistic and Christian ideals of the College of Liberal Arts of Howard University and thus merits richly such recognition as the Alumni Award can give."

Lay Leaders

The evangelistic power of consecrated preachers has moved the gospel to all corners of the world. But one cannot discount the influence of consecrated and dedicated laymen in the development of the Adventist Church.

First church, of Washington, D.C., organized February 24, 1889, has the honor of being the oldest active black congregation of the denomination. It existed as an integrated church in its embryo days. Laymen of the blackest hues collaborated with those of the fairest skin in planning programs for the church. It was in this environment that Dr. James Howard, Eva's uncle, moved and operated.

On the other side of town, Ephesus—later to become Dupont Park church—was breeding a group of well-educated, sophisticated, but concerned laymen. The evangelist Elder P. G. Rodgers had a knack for making the Adventist message appealing to upper-class black Washingtonians.

As this new group flocked into the church, sitting under the dual shadow of the General Conference headquarters and the nation's capital, they watched events going on in the country around them and measured the events against those happening in their own church headquarters.

It disturbed them that certain Adventist institutions would not admit blacks, nor would the Review and Herald Publishing Association cafeteria permit them to eat there. They were concerned because Negroes did not have total participation in the program of the church, in spite of the fact that they were well-qualified, able, and quite willing.

Elder Rodgers continued to bring upper-class black people into the Ephesus church. It was not an ordinary congregation, for it contained a large percentage of independent businessmen, public school teachers, government workers, and Howard University graduates. But they could not participate in many denominational activities.

Dr. Dykes, along with J. L. Moran and other laymen, was particularly interested in seeing a black school in the North (or in the East). It would include a boarding academy and a totally accredited college. They were concerned that their children had to travel so far south to Oakwood, and also felt that Adventists should have an academic presence in the nation's capital or near it. The fact that their children were denied access to other Adventist higher education facilities bothered them.

After the founding of the Washington Union School, Eva desired to see a totally accredited college in Washington. A letter from the former pastor who had baptized her and her mother shows how diligently she worked for this ideal.

> "1207 W. 98th Street
> "Los Angeles, California
> "September 10, 1929

"Dear Miss Dykes:

"Received your letter, also one from Professor

Moran, also the request for names on a petition. How I wish you had been here when I presented it. My, the crowd of people that rushed to the table at the front of the church to sign it was a strong testimony of the way the folks feel about the matter, and they will send their money in a little while.

"We are with you. Why, one might ask? Well, for thirteen years I've tried to beg the men at Washington, actually begged them, to help our colored boys and girls. I have many copies of memorials that I have sent and taken to General Conference meetings. All to no avail.

"I am sure that every honest colored believer throughout the United States feels that we cannot wait any longer for the men to do what Sister White said should have been done as soon as the Civil War ended. So arouse the folk everywhere, seek the Lord for guidance. Accept the counsel of earnest, interested, able colored leaders, and altogether working as one man, this project of justice, equity, and necessity will surely succeed. . . .

"Be of good courage. Press the battle to the front lines, for it will be a battle. Let us know just what you are doing there, and in a few weeks we will have a rally for the school in the East, and send all we can.

"I do not stretch the matter a bit when I say that the church here is loyal to the brethren and sisters in the East in their struggles, and we wish as a church to assure you of our prayers and our deep concern over the matter. Our personal love to you and all the brethren and sisters there, and be sure to write us often as to how you are succeeding. . . .

"The times are critical, and above all, may the Lord help us to press together, being first true to the loving Father above, and then true to each other.

"Yours for the Master
"P. G. Rodgers"

On July 7, 1941, Dr. Dykes received a letter from
the College of Medical Evangelists' School of Nursing
stating, "We are very sorry that we have no place in
our school for your niece, Anita M. Simms. Our
classes for this fall are made up, and we have a long
waiting list of students to fill any possible vacancies.
We find ourselves in a position that makes it
impossible for us to accept colored students."

The director explained that the other schools with
whom they affiliated would not accept black students
and thus CME could not give them full work and
graduate them. The incident inspired her to continue
working quietly in hopes of founding the black school
in the East. Later she sent her nephew Milton and
niece Jamie to Oakwood. But she continued to write,
and even got an opportunity to visit General Conference president J. L. McElhany to place her case for a
black school in the East before him. J. L. Moran had
found a farm outside Harrisburg, Pennsylvania, but
the school did not materialize then.

In the fall of 1943 a spark ignited the already-smol-
dering flames of dissatisfaction.

Three sober women climbed out of the little black
Model T Ford parked in front of Dodson's bookstore.
An onlooker would have supposed that the three
teachers had come to the college store at 2610 Georgia
Avenue to buy supplies for their students. When they
entered they went beyond the shelves and the stacks
of books and into a back room where ten others had
already gathered. After a few minutes of conversation,
tall Joe Dodson stood up, cleared his voice, had
prayer, and began to present the main item of

business for the evening.

His father, mother, and five brothers were always involved in some kind of political, social, intellectual, or religious discussion, and so his right to chair the discussion of this group had been earned, even in his childhood home.

He explained the problem. "Lucy Byard, a light-skinned mulatto from New York, was brought to the Washington Sanitarium during an illness. She was accepted by phone. They later informed her husband that the information he had placed on the admittance forms indicated that her racial identity was not white. Lucy Byard was wheeled into the hall while the sanitarium switchboard attempted to locate another hospital that would admit her. By the time she was finally taken to Freedman's Hospital she died of pneumonia."

Shocked by the news, the thirteen laypeople quickly organized themselves into the Committee for the Advancement of Worldwide Work Among Colored Seventh-day Adventists. Alma Scott served as its vice president.

Dodson continued to explain. "We are concerned that our children cannot enroll in Washington Missionary College, and we cannot eat in the Review and Herald cafeteria. The white members who had worshiped with the original members of First church have slowly moved away into their own churches, leaving First church an all-black church. First church and Ephesus often welcome visiting white ministers who pass by to deliver special messages on Sabbath, but they do not invite our ministers to their pulpits.

"Our aim is not segregation, but integration. None of us are militant. None of us are carrying banners or screaming. We are speaking our minds quietly, decently, intelligently. We are not threatening to leave the church, but we want to pull within the structure to see that all God's children are integrated into the programs that the church offers."

Smaller committees began to work. The group consisted of Willie Anna and Joseph T. Dodson, Alma J. Scott, Myrtle Murphy, Alan A. Anderson, J. Barnett, Dr. Eva B. Dykes, Dr. Valerie O. Justiss Vance, Dr. Grace Kimbrough, Dr. J. Mark Cox, James Montgomery, Addison Pinkney, and Helen Sugland.

Eva Dykes and some of the other women known for their writing ability began to hone out an eight-page statement of the committee's objectives. Others began to telephone across the country.

The group laid plans to inform Seventh-day Adventist blacks across the nation of their goals. They printed stationery and dispatched letters. Knowing that black church employees might lose their jobs if openly identified with the new movement, the lay-people moved to the front and spearheaded the drive.

Dr. Dykes spoke up. "I think we should send some representatives to see Elder McElhany. When I was interested in the school in the North, Helen Sugland and I visited Elder McElhany at the General Conference, and he listened very attentively to our request."

Heads nodded. The thirteen-member lay group managed to contact Elder McElhany about their concerns on the problem. He promised that he would study it and meet with them.

As a result of their contact, black leaders from various places in the United States convened in Chicago during April, 1944, to discuss the progress of black Adventism. Although not officially invited, a number of the members of the lay group traveled to Chicago and even though unsuccessful at the first meeting, Joe Dodson and Addison Pinkney—at that time a teacher—did finally succeed in seeing Elder McElhany. In that half-hour conference they presented the main points of their eight-page pamphlet.

Even though Elder McElhany became sick later on during the meeting, Elder G. E. Peters, then the secretary of the Colored Department of the General Conference, did manage to visit his bedside and lay the problem once again on his broad shoulders.

Leaving his sickbed, Elder McElhany chaired the meeting with the black delegates, and they took a vote that when the black constituency became large enough, and their financial income sufficient, colored conferences would be organized and administered by black officers and committees, and would have the same relationship to the union as did similar white conferences.

It was with great hesitancy that many discussed this question about leaving and separating, but realizing that it would provide blacks with job opportunities and experience, they voted to organize the Lake Region Conference on September 26, 1944. The new organization with J. G. Dassent as president began operating January 1, 1945. One week later the Northeastern Conference organized, and during 1945 the Allegheny Conference came into existence.

J. H. Wagner, president of the Allegheny Conference, invited the black members to its first camp meeting under all-black leadership. According to Jacob Justiss, "the Allegheny camp meeting of 1946 was the greatest gathering of Negro Seventh-day Adventists since the Oakwood Youth Congress, May 25-28, 1934. The preaching was superb. The singing with Eva B. Dykes directing the choir and with Sister Leona Meredith and Sister Wilhemina Waters presaging C. L. Brooks and Joyce Bryant was heavenly. Mae Justiss and Alice Brantley at the piano made all music sound well. The big yellow tent was full at all times in spite of the incessant downpour. Benches along the old wire fence were greeting places for long-separated friends. It was a great spiritual and social success."—*Angels in Ebony,* p. 112.

No one knew at that time that the planning being done in that back room by those thirteen members would result in the development of organizations that by 1983 totaled more than 150,000 members.

Later Dr. Dykes had the satisfaction of seeing her hopes for a school in the North materialize with the founding of Pine Forge Academy in Pennsylvania in 1946.

Onward to Oakwood

The Radcliffe class of 1917 published a twenty-fifth reunion book in 1942 describing the careers of its members since they had graduated. The women talked about their affiliations with various boards, libraries, art guilds, festivals, publications, and associations.

The Adventist Church captured the center of Eva B. Dykes's life. She mentioned it in her very first sentence.

"Since I left Radcliffe, I have enjoyed very much working in the Adventist Church in various capacities. I have found especial pleasure in visiting hospitals, childrens' homes, the old folks' home, and other institutions, either with literature or in singing groups. During vacations, I have derived joy from 'seeing America' by automobile, the trips having included visits to Massachusetts, Ohio, Alabama, North Carolina, Missouri, and Indiana. My trip in 1940 was the climax, a cross-country trip by automobile to California, where I was moved by the beauty, grandeur, and variety of nature—the great national parks of the West, its huge mountains, interesting rock formations, and lonely deserts.

"Especially fond am I of children and youth. To watch them grow and develop, and to see the varying characteristics of youth, especially those of college age, is enlightening. I have one of the dearest Sabbath school classes in the world—children from 11 to 14 years of age.

"I like life and people, and most of all, living. If I could afford it, I would retire and live in the country, where I spend at least part of my time every summer. The quiet there does something to one!"

Her driving skills had improved, and it was always a joy for her to take an excursion in her Model A Ford. Often dust would cover her black shiny car as she returned from the countryside. Sometimes she journeyed alone, but most often she traveled with her friends from the Ephesus church, Joe and Willie Dodson, Helen Sugland, and Myrtle Murphy. Many times she went with groups—her choirs, her classes, her young people. She was always active, always involved in life.

In the 1930s the majority of Oakwood's faculty remained white. Following a strategically timed student strike in 1932, the students requested that J. L. Tucker be the last white president. The predominantly white board acceded, and J. L. Moran became Oakwood's first black president. His goal was to create an outstanding black staff.

Elder Moran had often tried to get Eva to come to teach at Oakwood, but her uncle advised her that she probably could do more good for the church where she was.

A letter written May 10, 1934, by J. L. Moran mentions, "I just cannot tell you how much it would mean to the institution to have your able services. So remember, we are counting on you to accept the call." Apparently it was not convenient for her at that time to accept.

Another letter, June 15, 1934, from him appeals to her, "The board was very favorable to working out plans to make it possible for you to be with us. They voted to invite you as normal director and principal of the academy. The plan which we spoke of in regards to salary, boarding, and having a small apartment can be worked out all right. You will be able to begin your work in January—trusting your mother will have a successful operation, and that her health may be much improved as a result of the operation."

She was not interested in administration. Her strong emphasis was the teaching of English, and being in the classroom. With prayerful hesitancy she declined the offer.

It was during this period that the great tragedy of her life occurred. Dr. Howard passed away. *The Advent Review and Sabbath Herald* of February 20, 1936, carried several paragraphs about this pioneer worker. The first paragraph said, "Funeral services for Dr. James H. Howard, who passed away January 6, 1936, at the Washington Sanitarium and Hospital, aged 74 years, were held Sabbath afternoon, January 11, at the First Seventh-day Adventist church. Burial followed at the Harmony Cemetery, Monday afternoon."

It continues, "Dr. Howard was a Christian gentleman. His inspiring life, his noble character, have left their impression not only on the church circle, but on all who were acquainted with him. . . . We feel confident that our brother sleeps in Jesus, awaiting the voice of the Life-giver."

The big house seemed lonelier now without her uncle's counsel and inspiration. Eva and Martha Ann were sometimes at a loss to know what to do. It was during this period that they learned to place their confidence more fully in the One who watches over His children, their heavenly Father. He was still guiding and still directing their paths.

Eva often invited friends and strangers to the house. She wanted to be social to save. The following story from Mrs. Alan Anderson shows the relationship of her social life to her religious life.

"My home was in Marion, Indiana, and it was there that I met my husband and his mother. Of course, he wasn't my husband at the time. But his mother found out that I was planning a trip to Washington, D.C., their home, so they gave me a list of names of their friends that I should get in touch with when I arrived. It would be better if I contacted some of them rather than staying in the YWCA, since I knew no one in the city.

"I contacted Dr. Eva B. Dykes as soon as I arrived. She said, 'Oh, I know just the place for you to stay. My sister Anita will be happy to have you stay with her while you are here in Washington.'

"I did find a most pleasant fellowship with her sister and her sister's children, and I stayed there for the whole ten days that I was in Washington. But Dr. Dykes was very unusual. She came over to her sister's and would take me to places at the university. She invited me down to have lunch with the teachers. And she drove me around to see the city. The night before I left she took me to the grocery store and bought me all kinds of fruits and raisins and just loaded me up with food for the train. So I said that if all Adventists are like these Adventists, and I am a perfect stranger, then I want to be one too.

"Eva was always very pleasant and entertained a lot in her home. She had a long dining table, and she would have it full every Sabbath.

"Knowing that I would spend many hours on the train going back, she offered me several books to read. I was not an Adventist at the time. One of the books she gave me was *Straightening Out Mrs. Perkins.* Also she gave me some *Youth's Instructors* and some other magazines. By the time I got back to Indiana the Sabbath was clear in my mind. Next I took Bible studies from a woman in the local church.

"I never will forget her for that little book *Straightening Out Mrs. Perkins.* As a matter of fact, I passed it on to other people. By the time I reached home, after the long train ride, I was a 'pretty good Adventist.' I was ready to get baptized."

Dr. Dykes's trip of 1940 to California allowed her to see more of the United States than she had ever seen before, and it also took her to Oakwood College. She had often heard of this institution in the South, but now she received an invitation to speak there.

The Huntsville, Alabama, *Times*, May 20, 1940, carried the following news article: "Graduation exercises for Oakwood Junior College, at which diplomas will be presented to forty-eight students, will be held at the college at eight o'clock tonight.

"The graduating class, one of the largest in the college's history, has representatives from nineteen States on its roll.

"Dr. Eva B. Dykes, of Howard University, Washington, D.C., will be the principal speaker tonight.

"The college's new administration building and auditorium, erected at a cost of approximately $35,000, was dedicated at two o'clock this afternoon.

"J. L. McElhany, of Washington, D.C., president of the World Conference of Seventh-day Adventists, delivered the dedication address.

"The new building is 75 feet wide and 130 feet

long. It is a two-story stone structure with a basement."

It was the first time a woman had delivered the commencement address to the graduating class of Oakwood. Although Eva was decked in her regal black doctoral robe, with two blue velvet panels on the front and three blue velvet bars on each sleeve, her message was beautiful in its simplicity. Dr. Dykes realized that while Oakwood did not possess all of the material things of which other institutions could boast, its young people had something infinitely superior, the opportunity to prepare for service that would lead men to so order their lives that they would be assured of citizenship in the world to come. It was the theme of her message.

Elder James L. Moran, the president, and Elder Calvin E. Moseley, the head of the religion department, tried to show her how much the college needed her. A desire stirred in her heart to give of her time and talent to the Adventist institution.

When she returned she wished she could discuss it with her uncle, who had advised her to witness where she was. But her thoughts returned again and again to the little school in the South where they had prayer before each class and where salvation was the theme of every lesson.

Often as Elder Moran passed through the city of Washington he would drop by the Dykes' home to visit with his friend, and always he attempted to persuade her to come to Oakwood.

Very wisely, President Moran invited her to speak once again at Oakwood. On May 21, 1944, she delivered the commencement address. Eva pointed out that the school was making history, and that as scholastic standards reached higher levels, greater things would be expected of its graduates. She reviewed its history. Their aim was "With heads unbowed, we face the future," and their motto, "Accepting life's challenges, we fight to win." When she returned to Washington, thoughts of Oakwood and its students would not leave her mind.

Dr. Dykes made Oakwood a matter of prayer and asked the Lord to give her a sign. She asked that she might have a fervent desire, a longing to go there, that nothing else could satisfy. Soon she began to feel dissatisfied with Howard University. Later when she contacted President Moran that she would accept his offer, all doubts disappeared.

She quickly sent a letter explaining her decision, and on June 6, 1944, she received his reply:
"Dear Dr. Dykes:

"We sincerely appreciated your presence on the campus during the commencement exercises. Your address was really beautiful. So many have remarked about it, not only from our group, but from our sister institution, the A&M College.

"Needless to say, I was overjoyed when I reached home from student promotional work in connection with the Florida camp meeting and read your letter. As I read it, I thought of Moses and his decision. I can plainly see and understand the financial sacrifice that will come to you as you enter the cause of God, but somehow it has always appeared to me that the individual who can lay aside something for the sake of Christ gets a joy unknown to others. I often wish I could give up more for the sake of Christ, who gave so much for me.

"I hadn't planned to be in Washington before late in the summer, but my plans can be altered. A good worker is hard to find, and if it calls for slightly changed plans on my part, I am only too happy to make the change. I am scheduled to be in Pittsburgh on June 24 and 25. I can either come through Washington on my way to Pittsburgh or I can return home from Pittsburgh by way of Washington.

"I cannot say yet which way will be possible because a board meeting is scheduled during the month of June, sometime between June 20 and June 30. How will it be if I write you just as soon as I learn the date and arrange definitely to come and see you?

"You asked when we wanted you; whether at the beginning of the year or at the second semester. Practically all of our courses begin in September, and we would like to have you in September. This would give you an opportunity to help organize the English courses and put the department in the order that you would like to have it. Since we are inviting you to head the department we shall expect you to take the lead in organizing it.

> "Sincerely,
> "J. L. Moran"

Her salary would be $41 a week. President Moran told her that he was receiving $42 a week and that the board insisted that the president make at least one dollar more than the teaching staff. "He told me that the school would take out of my salary my rent, my electricity, et cetera, and that would leave me only $25 a week to take care of food and other living expenses," she said later.

"Many thought I was making a mistake, but on the whole the response was favorable, and the church gave me their prayers and blessings. When I told the members that President Moran had informed me that I would have $25 left for food and other expenses each week, some of my coworkers said that they were going to send me some money to help with expenses. They, up to this moment, have never sent me anything, yet God has blessed me wonderfully.

"I have found that His promise is true and sure."

Leaving Howard meant parting from some of the best-known educators and black leaders in the world. She had stood side by side with Dr. Ralph Bunche, diplomat and U.N. mediator; Todd Duncan, world-famous baritone singer; Alain LeRoy Locke, who was the first colored man to be a Rhodes scholar; Charles Harris Wesley, former president of Wilberforce University; Ernest E. Just, a biologist of unusual fame; Camille Nickerson, concert artist and teacher; and Louis Vaughn Jones, a famous violinist. All of them were or had been Howard professors and her colleagues.

When she had finally made the decision, and the Spirit of God had impressed her that she could be of greater service at Oakwood than at Howard, she slowly picked up her pen and wrote a letter of resignation to Dr. Johnson. The following documents express the sadness of the president and the faculty for her departure:

"Recommendation #80

"Indefinite leave of absence of Eva B. Dykes, Associate Professor of English.

"Recommended that Eva B. Dykes, Associate Professor of English, be given indefinite leave of absence from the College of Liberal Arts, beginning September 1, 1944.

"Respectfully submitted,

"J. Sinclaire Price, Dean

"Justification for recommendation #80."

The following letter from Dr. Dykes would dramatize

the unusualness of this recommendation:

"I herewith submit my resignation from the faculty of the College of Liberal Arts of Howard University, to take effect at the end of the summer school session, 1944.

"Our only colored Adventist institution of higher learning, Oakwood College at Huntsville, Alabama, is being changed from a junior college to a senior college, and the president of this school has invited me to connect with the faculty of that institution.

"The school is a small school in a rural section and is by no means comparable to Howard University in material, equipment, and financial resources, including salaries.

"My association with the president, faculty, and student body of Howard University for the past fourteen years has been particularly pleasant. Especially grateful am I for your advice and encouragement, Dean Price. I leave my alma mater with great regret, yet with a pleasant memory of a most happy and fruitful experience.

"It is my earnest prayer that Howard will continue to be a potent influence in the lives of our youth."

"But the recommendation is born of an absolute and well-nigh indomitable sense of propriety. How can Dr. Dykes, an honored alumna, a genuine constituent of the faculty of the college, and an indigenous member of the university and neighboring community, possibly resign!

"Such action is logically inconceivable, and organically impossible. As well may a child essay to resign from its home and family as for her to part company with Howard University.

"Therefore, let us regard her departure as a

spiritual adventure; the answer to the 'still small voice,' a veritable mission; a religious imperative; a call to service—anything short of resignation, but denoting the choosing of what she considers 'the better part.'

"She is sacrificing personal comfort, professional security, an intellectually stimulating and culturally tolerable environment, and 'filthy lucre' for the seclusion of 'a small school in a rural section.' . . .

"The university owes her the courtesy and should accord her the honor and reward of refusing to recognize her formal resignation.

"Dr. Dykes is attempting to resign for *a call*. Against Howard University she has no complaint. Her stay here has been a happy one. But she must go as a missionary to her church school. So to her the fair thing to do is to resign.

"Incidentally, it is my request that the university accord her a 'post-humorous' promotion! It will be recalled that she led the list of those recommended by me for promotion in rank this year. Argument in support of this request will be fulsome and offensive if the foregoing plea has any merit.

"Respectfully submitted,
"J. St. Clair Price
"Dean"

She would always be a daughter of Howard and a friend of the institution. As Dr. Johnson put it in his letter: "Our prayers will follow you wherever you may go."

"August 26, 1944

"Dr. Eva B. Dykes
"1724 Eighth Street, NW.
"Washington, D.C.

"Dear Dr. Dykes:

"On behalf of the board of trustees, faculties, administrative officers, students, and all the members of the Howard University staff, it gives me pleasure, mingled with sadness, to send greetings to you on this occasion.

"You have served as a member of the faculty of the College of Liberal Arts, in the Department of English, over a long period of years. You have done your work with intelligence, with constructiveness, and with honor. By your training and competence, by your pioneering vision and faith, your devotion to the highest ideals, your single-minded, undiscourageable and uncalculating labors, you have come to be an inspiring leader in the cause of education for all the people.

"You have loved your students, you have held your colleagues in reverent esteem, and you have been a center of cooperating loyalty to your alma mater, which has been beautiful to behold.

"In the strength of your mind, the repose of your self-respect, the buoyancy of your goodwill, the integrity of your relations, you are an inspiring example of the essential dignity and the highest possibilities of the human soul.

"The influence of your life in the Howard University community will go on working. Our prayers will follow you wherever you may go.

"God bless you and keep you and give you the much-needed strength for the tasks that lie ahead.

"Sincerely yours,

"Mordecai W. Johnson
"President"

Now it was onward to Oakwood.

Audibility and Academics

The train snaked its way around mountains and through valleys. Scores and scores of unfamiliar towns crawled by. New passengers climbed in and old ones struggled out. Burnt-red roads intersected the countryside. The air became stifling, but the conductor continued to rattle off unfamiliar names of little towns as they continued southward. At last he shouted, "Huntsville!"

Stiff from the ride, Pum Pum rose slowly, and Eva, between handling the baggage and holding onto the side of the car, tried to help her mother off the coach.

In 1944 Huntsville had a population of fourteen thousand. The two women waited in the segregated waiting room until someone from the college came to escort them to their lodging. They walked around the tiny colored waiting room and took a drink from the colored drinking fountain.

At last their escort arrived. "See that building there?" he questioned as he drove from the train station to the college. "That's the little Huntsville Negro Library. It houses just a few books." Eva realized it was true because the little frame building didn't have the capacity to hold too many volumes. "There's a larger Huntsville library, but not available to those 'from Oakwood.'"

"That's our hospital. If you ever get sick, you'll have to enter through the rear door and be treated in the small rear wing specifically sectioned off for colored patients." They came to the town square. "These drinking fountains are for 'colored'; these are for 'white,'" he pointed out. Pum Pum had a terrific headache, a combination of the long trip and the thought of leaving her beloved Washington, D.C. She had been ill over the past few years, and the move would be a difficult one for her.

Oakwood had been established in 1896. When social difficulties broke out in the Southland in the 1890s, Ellen G. White instructed the denomination to establish an institution to train blacks to work for their own people.

In 1895 the General Conference sent a three-man educational committee to Tennessee and Alabama to select and purchase a property not to exceed $8,000 for a school for black youth. They learned of the 360-acre Irving farm in northern Alabama, and after making their report to headquarters, returned to negotiate for the purchase of the land. The mother of the agent handling the property had been a patient at the Battle Creek Sanitarium. Through this favorable contact they bought the land for $6,700, a thousand dollars less than the original asking price.

Huntsville was then a town of seven thousand citizens. Founded in 1805 by John Hunt, of Virginia, it bore his name. Afterward it took the name "Twickenham" to honor the home of the poet Alexander Pope, since some of his relatives were among the early settlers. Later it was changed back to Huntsville. Today the research and work at Redstone Arsenal makes Huntsville the space capital of the world and has helped it to grow to more than 100,000.

Oakwood was founded to be a self-supporting work-learn institution. The spacious but dilapidated manor house already on the property served as classrooms and a dormitory. Other structures included an old barn and a row of nine crumbling cabins. Five of the latter consisted of squared cedar logs planted upright in the ground and clapboarded.

O. A. Olsen and G. A. Irwin both returned in their overalls and worked to prepare the site. The first principal, Solon M. Jacobs, added an eighteen-by-forty-four-foot room to the manor house (Old Mansion) to serve as kitchen and dining hall. By November of 1896 the school had a new two-story building, the first floor used for classrooms and the second as a boys' dormitory. With these few buildings, four teachers, eight male students, and eight female students, Oakwood Industrial School opened its doors on November 16, 1896.

Over the years Oakwood added a few simple buildings, and soon the school consisted of Old Mansion (girls' dorm), the orphanage, Oaklawn, Butler Hall (boys' dorm), West Hall (dining hall), Henderson Hall (girls' dorm), the elementary school, the laundry, and the sanitarium. The first students worked on the farm in the daytime and studied their lessons at night.

For two decades Oakwood operated on the secondary level under the name Oakwood Industrial School, Huntsville Training School, and (1904) Oakwood Manual Training School. In April, 1917, the North American Division Council met on Oakwood's campus and elevated the status to Oakwood Junior College. In 1918 the first two students completed the two-year college course. Later the trustees purchased six hundred additional acres. Many veterans enrolled after World War II, and much of the timber on its land provided the material for ten barrack-type buildings.

Ellen G. White said in a speech at Oakwood on June 21, 1904, "It was God's purpose that the school should be placed here.

"He has bestowed on the colored race some of the best and highest talents. . . . You have precious opportunities here [in this school]."

The year before Eva's arrival the school had legally dropped "junior" from its name, and now it was the Oakwood Senior College. Unaccredited, unattractive, the fledgling institution boasted an enrollment of 344 and a faculty of fourteen. Dr. Dykes would be the head of an English department that had one other teacher (Garland J. Millet, who later became president), and would be the first teacher holding a doctorate at the institution. She would see the first Bachelor's degrees of Oakwood Senior College conferred on its students by J. L. Moran.

The car drove five miles along the dusty road and stopped before a two-story white building. The porch creaked as they walked across it. A weak light bulb over the front door managed to reveal patches of peeling paint and a sign that said East Hall.

The wooden clapboard building had been erected in 1909 under the inspiration of Ellen G. White, who called for the expansion of medical services among blacks in the South. It was dedicated as the sanitarium and nurses' training center under the direction of Dr. M. M. Martinson. Later it became East Hall, the girls' dormitory. In 1938 the school remodeled it as the home for Elder J. L. Moran, the first black president of Oakwood College.

Just prior to her arrival the college had built a new home of stone down the road for Elder Moran, and now the college's first doctorate received the old president's house. From 1944 until 1965 the first floor of East Hall would be the residence of Dr. Eva B. Dykes. Other teachers would live on the upper floor.

In 1967, the college renovated East Hall to house the behavioral science center. Today it stands as the oldest building on the Oakwood campus, housing the credit union and the church mission office.

Word quickly passed that Dr. Dykes had arrived on campus. The students were quite eager to see the great and learned teacher from Howard, the North's most prestigious black school. But it was with great disappointment that they first glimpsed the newcomer.

"She's wearing nothing but a washable gingham dress," one girl moaned.

"She doesn't look like a doctor to me!" another student volunteered.

"She's so little and ordinary," someone remarked.

Dr. Dykes has herself commented that "whenever I read or hear what people have to say about me, I wonder upon what they base their remarks. I am so very ordinary."

But it was such a down-to-earth spirit, combined with her gracious manner, her intellectual attainment, and her Christian character, that combined to make her a great teacher. She determined that all who would leave her classes would be less dumb, less deaf, less blind, less ignorant. During the next few weeks she showed that even though she was small, she was tough, and even though she was not pretentious in dress, she was perfectly capable in the classroom.

Eva enjoyed the view of the mountains surrounding East Hall and their thickly wooded slopes. But her mother's health seemed to grow worse. After enduring patiently a lingering illness, she fell asleep in Jesus about 4:00 A.M., May 12, 1945. Before she went into her coma, her last words were "Eva, you've been a good daughter to me."

It was a new thing for Dr. Dykes to be at a school where they had prayer before each class. She liked it. After prayer that first day of class she explained her program. "Students," she said, "I have high standards, I have two A's that I stress. 'A' for academic excellence and mastery of subject matter, but I also have an 'A' that stands for audibility. Everything that is said must be said so that I and those around you, your fellow students, will hear it.

"If you speak and no one hears you, what you have said is of no value. No matter how correct the answer, no matter how good the response, it is worthless. I must insist that you speak audibly. Audibility, students."

During the first week they began to realize the importance of her two A's.

She stood for excellence and saw it as her responsibility to acquaint her students with it. When she recognized that a student had good potential, she required more of him than of those who were struggling. Many became acquainted with the concept of bonehead English.

"No one has done well on her tests; no one has spoken loudly and clearly enough for her," some students groaned.

"We have A's, but they don't stand for good work, just audibility," others complained.

"She has such high standards."

"She couldn't possibly flunk the whole class," someone volunteered. But she did exactly that.

The first nine weeks produced much weeping and

wailing and gnashing of teeth. She gave so much homework, trying to increase their level of knowledge and good English usage, that the students decided to do something about it. One day they arrived for class, each carrying a large suitcase. When the bell rang, each student calmly walked into the room and placed his suitcase on top of the desk.

She apparently didn't observe, or if she did, overlooked the incident and calmly began the teaching of her lesson. When she called for the homework assignments all forty or so suitcases clicked open, and the students with great dramatic flair removed their assignments from the recesses of the suitcases and brought them up to the front.

Few realize the tremendous task a black college has. Many of its students come from ghetto areas with families who place little emphasis on culture, learning, or correct grammar. Surviving is a full-time job. Harvard, Yale, and the so-called better schools produce their brilliant scientists and statesmen, but they allow only the cream of the crop to enter. Their entrance requirements are so stringent that they accept only the best. But Oakwood and its sister black institutions had to accept any and all who wanted an education. That it supplied all the numerous early ministers and leaders of black Adventism, that so many left to serve so admirably and competently, is a miracle.

No one is sure where the motto came from, but it graces the front pages of many of the Oakwood College bulletins. Its message is inscribed over the doors of several of the buildings. "Enter to Learn, Depart to Serve," it declares.

Dr. Dykes saw to it that every student who entered Oakwood came to learn, if not in all the other subjects, at least in English. Because she and her colleagues cared, Oakwood has sent hundreds of students to all parts of the world to serve the church and to carry the message of Adventism.

In the book that she later coauthored with Florence M. Winslow, called *The Manual of English*, she aptly describes why every student should develop the ability to write. In the introduction she stated, "Why should you learn writing? Out of the Elizabethan period comes Francis Bacon with an answer. 'Writing maketh an exact man.' It is as though he looked down the centuries to see this space age in which a miscalculation of a fraction of an inch could throw a missile thousands of miles off course, and who would bear the blame?

"Who, but the man whose writing was not exact. In freshman composition, aside from writing, you will also do an extensive amount of reading. Again, Francis Bacon speaks. 'Reading maketh a full man.' You students must fill yourselves with a variety of worthwhile selections, with an eye single to developing your own styles and writing.

"This does not necessarily mean that you will become a Shakespeare, but you will gain the pleasure of feeling that your writing will have lifted itself out of mediocrity. You can gain this increased skill only through contact with the greatest minds, contact gained to the greatest extent through reading."

More than twenty-three years of teaching black students had prepared her for Oakwood. Many wondered how she could leave the convenience and beauty of the capital city for an undeveloped, unaccredited school. But a Higher Power had guided and led her to Oakwood College.

Many administrators from renowned schools

across the country tried to lure her away from Oakwood with offers of larger pay, greater benefits, or better working and living conditions. The Board of Education of the City of St. Louis asked her to fix her own salary. A Western Union telegram from Tuskegee Institute urged her to leave Oakwood "to offer valuable assistance" there.

Administrators who chanced to meet her at educational meetings came away impressed and sought her services. An official from Florida A & M University wrote, "I was very pleased to have had the opportunity of meeting you at the recent meeting of the Association of Colleges and Secondary Schools.

"As indicated to you, I am particularly interested in securing the services of outstanding persons to work here on the faculty, and we would be certainly interested to have you consider the possibility of employment here."

When Dr. Jackson, director of the College of Arts and Sciences of Wilberforce University in Ohio, wrote that "President Westly is particularly interested in having you come to our faculty here," she replied, as always, "I am on permanent tenure at Oakwood."

Where Loveliness Keeps House

Dr. Dykes' influence grew like one of the many oak trees scattered over Oakwood's campus. At first small, they continued to develop until they towered above many buildings, and their shadows fell across the students and the campus.

President Garland J. Millet, in a tribute he paid to Dr. Dykes, spoke of her impact on all who came into contact with her.

"When she went to Oakwood from Howard, at personal sacrifice, in 1944, the college was in its infancy as a senior institution. In fact, it took much faith, foresight, and courage for President Moran to promote the plan!

"Consequently, there was much to be desired both in available facilities and in the program, and very little money to work with. But Dr. Dykes is a lamplighter. We think of the five thousand gas lamps still in London, and some indeed with pilot lights and time switches, but others that require a lamplighter with a torch on a long pole, 'going around' to light each lamp.

"So instead of bemoaning the conditions, she *lighted lamps!* With her glowing faith and infectious optimism, she vigorously supported the program of Christian education, typically and literally, giving it all she had.

"She is a booster, a cooperator, and a leader. Her energy, love, understanding, and skill have supported six presidents for more than a quarter of a century at Oakwood."

She went vigorously to work fulfilling all the requests of every chief administrator of the institution. Her first summer there she recruited students. Many pastors received letters like this one from Dean O. B. Edwards, written to Elder J. H. Laurence, June 13, 1945:

"Following the request of F. L. Peterson, we are sending Dr. Eva B. Dykes, formerly of Howard University, but now head of the English department of the Oakwood College, to your city.

"She would be very happy to have your cooperation in contacting former students and prospective students. She is expecting to arrive in Cleveland by July 3, and would be able to remain there until July 5. We are sure that you stand ready to lend your full cooperation in our plan, and the college will greatly appreciate all you may do."

Her influence on and off campus continued to grow. Six presidents of Oakwood—J. L. Moran, F. L. Peterson, G. J. Millet, A. V. Pinkney, F. W. Hale, Jr., and C. B. Rock—found this little lady a package of dynamite and energy. All would seek advice from her on important academic matters. She was ready to do whatever she was asked or whatever she thought should be done.

Her first year of activities, besides a full teaching load and administrative duties as chairman of the division of humanities, included sponsoring the senior class of Oakwood's first four-year graduates, delivering its presentation address in March, starting and sponsoring the English club, directing the school choir, and advising the two student publications, *The Spreading Oak* and *The Acorn.*

While doing all of this she continued to furnish monthly articles to *Message* magazine. She saw to it that the English department added additional courses, and she taught an amazingly large variety of classes: composition, grammar, journalism, methods of teaching English, world literature, American literature, and every period course in English literature.

To keep abreast with what was happening in her profession she attended institutes and workshops and professional meetings. At many of them she participated on panel discussions or read papers. Once she took a correspondence course on eastern antiquities.

Studying one summer under Owen Thomas at Indiana University, she helped prepare *A Manual for a Beginning Teacher of Linguistics in a Secondary School.* She saw to it that her faculty had opportunities for improvement and often requested the chief administrator or the dean to work out financial arrangements for certain teachers who wanted to attend professional meetings or take study leave.

Whenever new teachers arrived on campus, she trained them to be of the highest service. If she heard an idea or saw an innovation that could be implemented at her own institution, she would gladly bring it back.

One visit to Southern Missionary College motivated her to start a campuswide English improvement program that she directed for many years. Called "English Cooperation," it involved every teacher on the campus in the task of improving student writing. Dr. Dykes supervised the production of a little manual that she put into the hand of every teacher and student. After observing the alumni files at Southern Missionary College, she began organizing and procuring file cabinets to list for the first time the names of Oakwood graduates alphabetically and according to classes.

The administration asked her to chair many of the college activities. She coordinated all social activities for faculty, students, and special occasions. In addition she selected lyceum artists and previewed motion pictures brought on the campus by student organizations and other related activities.

Her passion for Ingathering had not diminished over the years, and the administration soon noticed her ability to raise funds and inspire others to do the same. Garland J. Millet shares one little anecdote: "One time in the long ago, in preparation for a fund-raising drive at Oakwood College, I sponsored one team and challenged Dr. Dykes to lead the other one. I remember part of her introduction speech given in public, perhaps at an Oakwood chapel. She stated, 'President Millet has challenged me, *me*, to this contest in fund raising.' Her team succeeded in bringing in more funds than her humbled opponent accumulated."

Often she would push the drive to its conclusion during the Christmas season. She continued to contact her friends back at Howard University. A letter dated November 22, 1972, from her former Howard president not only included greetings and thanks for a copy of *Message* magazine, but also his annual check of $50.

"Dear Miss Dykes:

"Please let me thank you for the beautiful copy of

Message. Mrs. Johnson and I will read it with eager interest.

"We are very happy indeed to see your name again with your inspiring connection with Oakwood. We both hope that you are well and going on as usual with your greatly meaningful work.

"Herewith, I send my check for $50 to help support the medical, education, and Christian uplift that the Oakwood College church is doing. We hope that our very small contribution may be of some help. I remember you warmly from the days when you were at Howard.

"Sincerely,

"Mordecai Johnson"

Her home was a Bethany for many of the administrators, a place of warmth and friendship. Everyone knew that if you wanted to find her early in the morning, you had to go around back to her enclosed porch where she slept at night to get all of the fresh air that God could provide.

Often she rose at four o'clock in the morning to make plans for her classes and for the committees that she chaired. She continued practicing her piano at six o'clock in the morning.

Many times when she needed to raise money for facilities at Oakwood and she found that the board members were dragging their feet, she would invite them to her home and serve them breakfast. While she was eating she would lecture them from her prepared notes on the need for immediate action and would outline in 1, 2, 3 order what she felt they ought to do.

The faculty often called upon her to lead the students in the Oakwood song. Dr. Otis B. Edwards, the dean of the college, had written it, and would frequently play the piece. He would have them draw out the last syllables, "Here we spent our happy days, so we love to sing thy praise," and then as the rapid cadence would return, the students would blend their voices and sing out, "Worthy dear old O.C."

Oakwood College Song

Our dear Oakwood within whose vale
Thy standards will not fail,
Our hearts are filled with wondrous cheer
When thoughts of thee draw near.
We love thy pines, thy elms, thy oaks
And campus always green,
Thy many flowers and distant mounts,
Form one impressive scene.
Chorus:
To thee our dear Oakwood
To thee we shall ever sing,
For decades thou hast stood
Thy name should ever ring.
Here we've spent our happy days
So we love to sing thy praise,
And wherever we may be
We'll always be true to thee
Our worthy, dear old O.C.

—Dr. O. B. Edwards

Accreditation and Europe

When Oakwood seriously considered accreditation, it called upon its first and at that time only doctor to head up the accreditation committee. During that time she inundated General Conference officials, conference board members, and faculty members with requests for help.

Then one day the bells began ringing, and classes came to an early end. Puzzled teachers checked their watches to discover if the problem lay with them or with the clocks on the walls. They soon learned that the administration had called a special chapel. Chapels generally met Monday, Wednesday, and Friday, and since December 4 was a Thursday, calling the meeting was definitely unusual.

The students found their seats. Dr. Edwards stood and the assembly automatically came to silence. Someone offered a prayer, and then Dr. Edwards called on college president Garland J. Millet to give the exciting news for the morning. The president announced that he had been informed that at ten-thirty-five that morning, December 4, 1958, Oakwood College had become accredited by the Southern Association of Colleges and Schools.

Many students did not realize the full impact of the announcement as they sang "To God Be the Glory," but for Oakwood it was a big step. Dr. Dykes's ready smile is pictured on the front row of the faculty group photograph taken at the celebration that followed, and the president, board, and faculty attempted to express their appreciation for her leadership by granting her a leave of absence. Dr. Millet apologized for the fact that the school could give only $400 worth of financial assistance toward her first trip to Europe. But she made arrangements with the airline for a credit of $2,100 so that her sister Anita could travel with her. Anita would meet her in New York.

Her diary recounts the trip:

"Elder Stafford on a bleak rainy day drove me to the Huntsville Airport where I was to board the plane for New York at 9:07 A.M. on my way to Europe. The plane was twenty-three minutes late. Principal Stafford who kindly waited to see me off had prayer with me. I boarded the plane, and every now and then I would wave Goodbye to him. Although he was busy, he was sympathetic enough to wait until my plane was ready to take off. He did not know that this gesture caused me to feel so hopelessly 'alone.'

"I am on the plane now. The hostess comes around to check the names of the passengers. We are still on the ground. Slowly and leisurely like a proud peacock the engine purrs (mixed metaphor), the wings spiral around. The plane struts ostentatiously down the runway until it approaches the turn. The hostess admonishes us to put on our seat belts. We learn that we will fly nine thousand feet high with the first stop at Knoxville, and that the flying time is exactly forty-three minutes.

"In a few minutes a complete metamorphosis has taken place. Instead of being confronted by a dull, drab day with rain intermittently falling, I am gradually transported into a Fairyland high above the clouds.

"I can see the blue of the sky and the warm sun shining from a cerulean dome. Completely hidden are the brown earth, the green trees, the cozy-looking cottages, the twisting streets checkered here and there with plots of green.

"This trip was a thrilling experience for me. The airline arranged our travel itinerary so that we would not be traveling on the Sabbath from sunset Friday to sunset Saturday. Thus, we were left free to attend church on two Sabbaths. On the third Sabbath we were abroad, we spent the day by a beautiful lake since there was no Seventh-day Adventist church in the city where we found ourselves. It was a pleasure to meditate upon the reflection of God in the beauty of nature.

"In England we visited some famous places, such as Dickens' Old Curiosity Shop, Piccadilly Circus, Trafalgar Square, Windsor Castle, and the Shakespeare country. We traversed the same road as Chaucer's Canterbury pilgrims took their famous pilgrimage to the shrine of Thomas à Becket, the martyr. Other famous places we visited in England were Westminster Abbey; the graveyard celebrated in Gray's 'Elegy'; the tower where Sir Thomas More, author of *Utopia*, was executed; Hampton Court, where a group of scholars was authorized by James I to translate the Bible, which became known as the Authorized Version.

"In France we visited the renowned Riviera, where sky and water vie with each other in making for themselves a covering of cerulean blue; Nice; Monte Carlo, home of Grace Kelly, who married the ruler of Monaco; Napoleon's tomb; and a statue of the peasant maid Joan of Arc.

"Then we visited Italy, including the famous Appian Way, Rome with its seven hills, and Venice, renowned for its canals and its association with Shakespeare's *Merchant of Venice.* Thence to Holland, London, and back to New York and good old U.S.A.!

"I shall always be grateful to the board for this moment of high adventure!"

Back at Oakwood she plunged with renewed vigor into her activities. How she found time for extracurricular activities was beyond belief, but she did. Although she worked quietly, she achieved much. She was president of the Oakwood College Faculty Women's Club, and she organized a sorority for Oakwood coeds, the Gamma Sigma Kappa, for the express purpose of enhancing the cultural interests of the young women of the junior and senior classes. The club stressed better womanhood by emphasizing honesty, purity, and other praiseworthy traits. The motto of the club was "Honesty, fidelity, and courage." Dr. Dykes wrote the music for their theme song.

The expression "Oakwood is the place where loveliness keeps house," adapted from the Southern poet Madison Cawein, became popular on campus. Now Oakwood was becoming a lovelier-looking place, both in its physical characteristics and also in its student body. During Christmas of 1946, Dr. Dykes's choir performed Handel's *Messiah,* starting an Oakwood tradition that lasts even today.

Dr. Dykes was the first teacher requested after neighboring Alabama A & M University arranged a cooperative exchange of teachers in 1961. Later she taught part-time there for several years. Also she found time to be active in the community and serve as head of the Oakwood Chapter of the National Temperance Society. She chaired the Mother's March for the March of Dimes during the 1960s, writing and circulating a letter on the accomplishments of the foundation.

World War II was still in progress when Dr. Dykes left Washington. The students who came the first few years of her tenure there were older, mature individuals receiving Veterans Administration grants. They came with families and lived in special areas for married students. The college required students to show they had brought their own sugar and food rations before it allowed them to register.

Rarely did she insist on being called Dr. Dykes. It seemed as if those who knew her felt constrained to refer to her as that. The only place that she required her title was when she went to Huntsville. She remembers visiting the post office or the train station where those in charge spoke to her as "Auntie," or used her first name. As a defense, whenever she went to town she would identify herself as "Dr. Dykes, chairman of the English department of Oakwood College."

Sometimes she found herself being discriminated against just because she was a woman. When she arrived at Oakwood she earned $41 a week. One day as she passed Moran Hall she heard one of the professors thanking President Peterson for the raise that he had received. Quickly Dr. Dykes approached the administrator and asked him about the raise. Then she inquired further as to why she had not received hers.

"But Dr. Dykes," he told her with a conciliatory gesture, "you are a woman." Always quick with a retort, she said, "Elder Peterson, when I go to the store to buy food or books, do they charge me less because I am a woman? Does it cost me less because I am a woman?" Her arguments unfortunately did not produce the desired increase.

On Controversial Issues

Except for those few years at Radcliffe in Massachusetts, Dr. Dykes lived and worked, attended school, and taught south of the Mason-Dixon line. It was inevitable that a life of 90 years should bring her into contact with prejudice, discrimination, and hatred. But she was never bitter or faultfinding. Her intellectual attainments did not alter her gracious manner, her kindly spirit, her simplicity and humility, her Christian character.

From a portion of an unpublished interview conducted by Dr. Jannith Lewis, librarian of Oakwood College, we get insights into the philosophy of civil rights and Christian brotherhood. The interview took place September 5, 1973, in the residence of Dr. Dykes at Oakwood College.

DR. LEWIS: "Have you been active or involved in any manner with civil rights activities?"

DR. DYKES: "When Martin Luther King emphasized the civil rights movement some years ago, I was at Oakwood College. The Oakwood College church as a body was not involved. But a few teachers and students of the college did participate. And I have known of various adult individuals of the Seventh-day Adventist Church who were active in the movement.

"My personal involvement has been confined to the fervent hope and prayer that some of the deplorable conditions among all minority groups might be remedied. I was once a member of the NAACP, and also subscribed to its magazine *The Crisis*. Some years ago I was a member of the SDA layman's group that had as its objective better recognition of blacks in the SDA movement as a whole. It sought not only the holding of responsible positions in the black or regional conferences, but in the General Conference. In recent years blacks have been vice presidents of the General Conference and associate leaders in various areas such as education, temperance, and the like."

DR. L. "What was life for you like before the period of extensive civil rights legislation?"

DR. D. "I would like to preface my remarks by saying that I was fortunate to have a Christian mother and a Christian uncle who influenced considerably my attitude toward prejudice among the blacks. My uncle and mother did not have a militant spirit, but they would always emphasize the fact that prejudice did more damage to those who were prejudiced than to those against whom they discriminated.

"At first this seemed a little difficult for me to understand, but as I attended the Sabbath school in the First church of Washington, D.C., I learned more and more about the forgiving, kindly nature of Christ, the Master Teacher; of one of His seven last words, 'Father, forgive them; for they know not what they do'; and that although we might be wounded and grieved because of injustice, we should have the spirit of the meek and lowly Jesus.

"You will probably recall that He showed righteous indignation in driving out of the Temple the money changers who were desecrating it, but He never used violence against those who mistreated Him.

"I think the Negro spiritual 'crucifixion' aptly expresses this idea: 'They nailed Him to the tree, an' He never said a mumbalin' word. Not a word, not a word, not a word.'

"Since I was born in a Southern city, Washington, D.C., I attended only black schools: a black elementary school, a black high school, and a black college, Howard University.

"I recall that while I was at Howard, the students objected to the singing of Negro spirituals because they were reminiscent of the days of slavery. Also while I was young there was a race riot in Washington, D.C., that was very painful, not only to the blacks but also to the liberal whites. Another experience I had was on my first train trip to the Southland, when I had to ride in a Jim Crow car. This experience brought tears to my eyes. I cried not from anger, but from sorrow. The Jim Crow car was directly behind the engine, which threw back its smoke and fine coal dust into the hot, crowded, small coach.

"At first Pullman service was denied to blacks, but later they could ride in a Pullman with whites, but not in a coach with them. In the early days blacks had to bring their lunches and eat them in the crowded, hot, dusty Jim Crow coach. Later they could eat in a dining car, but were shunted off to a corner where a curtain enclosed them and shut them off from the whites in the other portion of the diner.

"Another incident of prejudice occurred during the time I was attending Radcliffe and a friend of mine was at Howard. We stopped at a restaurant in New York City. Whenever we put our money into the slot, it always came out again. We kept trying for a while, but finally decided to give up on the machine. Then we saw that it would work for the whites. However, when we returned and tried it, something would go wrong.

"I also remember when I was a little girl, my mother would take us for a Sunday ride to a recreational facility on the outskirts of Washington. Blacks could ride to the entrance, but could not enter. This fact, however, did not prevent us from enjoying the ride.

"Many theaters in Washington were in those days closed to blacks. My sister and a friend went several times to the old National Theater, which would not admit blacks. My sister, with her fine features and beautiful brown skin, dressed as an East Indian in bright colors and sparkling jewelry, while her friend was probably thought to be Portuguese. They had no difficulty in entering or being seated.

"Certain hospitals and diners in D.C. were denied to blacks. However, I went to one of these hospitals once to have my tonsils removed. While it would admit whites to the beautiful spacious main building, I had to stay overnight in one of the small frame buildings.

"Blacks could not even buy at Woodward and Lothrop, one of the main department stores in Washington, D.C. But now they no longer refuse the patronage of blacks. Early experiences like these remind me of the unforgettable language of Langston Hughes, who wrote words to this effect: 'Life for me ain't been no crystal stair, it's had many hard tacks.' During experiences like these I would always feel sorrow for those who were driving the hard tacks into the lives of the blacks.

"Just one more experience. When I was working on my doctorate at Radcliffe, my professor at Howard University wrote to the historical society of one of the Carolinas to see whether I could visit to do some research. He received an answer stating that they did not admit colored students for any type of research."

DR. L. "I understand that at the post office at one time you found it expedient to use your academic title 'Dr.' because it was the custom of the people to refer to black women by their first name or by the term 'Auntie.'"

DR. D. "That is true. When I first came to this State to teach, the train station down on Church Street had waiting rooms for blacks and whites. There were separate libraries. The one for black people was a small, white frame building on Church Street, which had only a few books compared with the library for the whites. The Huntsville Hospital had one small wing for the colored patients in the rear.

"The black students from Oakwood who did missionary activities would work only for the blacks in this hospital, and could enter only by the rear door. They could not enter the front door at all. In the stores in Alabama, I recall fountains with the words 'Colored' over one fountain and 'White' over another."

DR. L. "On the referring to people by their names, I also heard a little incident about the fact that a local businessman referred to one of your colleagues from Oakwood College as 'Professor,' rather than 'Mister,' even though he was not a professor."

DR. D. "Well, I could understand why the person said

the word 'Professor.' The word 'Mister' is another name for '*magister*,' the Latin form for 'master,' and the white man, probably in his subconscious mind, never wanted to acknowledge that the colored man was his master. And this to me was one of the reasons why the colored man was always addressed as 'Professor' and never as 'Mister.'"

DR. L. "Have you played a role or contributed to the area of civil rights in Alabama or black history?"

DR. D. "My contribution toward civil rights in Alabama and black history may be stated in this way: I have tried to do my best in whatever field I found myself, to make the wonderful mind that God has given man, a kingdom in itself. I say this with apologies to Sir Edward Dyer, the Elizabethan poet, who wrote, 'My mind to me a kingdom is.' Also I recall words in Milton's *Paradise Lost*, 'The mind is its own place, and in itself can make a heaven of Hell, a hell of Heaven.' If the mind can be filled with the best thoughts and with the desire to do one's best in whatever direction it may move, the black experience can be one of love to all mankind, and the living exemplification of the command of Christ who said we must let our lives be governed by two principles—a deep love for God and a deep love for our neighbor, which must be equal in scope and intensity to our love for ourselves."

Dr. L. "What is your overall opinion of the developments that have been made in the black struggle socially, educationally, or culturally?"

DR. D. "My overall opinion is that the black man has

come a long way in the past two or three decades. We see more black faces in the newspapers, over the TV, in athletics, in books written by both blacks and whites, and in integrated schools. Such signs are encouraging. But in my opinion, these advances will never reach their highest fulfillment until the kingdoms of this world are superseded by the rule of Him whose kingdom will be one of love, joy, and peace forevermore."

Dr. L. "Just one more thing, Dr. Dykes. You were one of the three first black women awarded the Ph.D degree in 1921. You might have had, as a woman and as a black, some unique experiences in your preparation and training for this highest of academic degrees. Do you remember any one in particular?"

DR. D. "I remember an experience that I had while doing research for my Ph.D thesis. Morning after morning I would go to the Library of Congress and work on my thesis. One day when I looked up, I saw the face of a young Japanese standing over me. He said to me, 'Will you pardon my intrusion, but I have seen you come in here repeatedly day after day, and you stay here until nine o'clock at night working, and I was wondering exactly what you were doing.' 'I am working on my doctorate at Radcliffe College,' I explained. 'Well, I'm working on mine too,' he replied, 'and maybe we could talk together about our experiences. What about our having lunch together?'

"My mother had taught me to be careful around men. But I could see something in him that led me to believe that he was a true gentleman. 'Certainly, we shall eat lunch together,' I told him. So we went out one day. And he said, 'Shall we go to one of the restaurants around the library?' 'I am not permitted to go into the library's,' I explained. 'I have my own lunch.' This fact hurt him. I suppose he hadn't been over here in the United States too long, and he probably didn't know much about the racism that existed at that particular time.

"As I said before, he was so hurt, or seemed hurt, by this fact, that he said to me, 'I am not going into any of these restaurants either.' Then he added, 'May I eat lunch with you?' And I replied, 'Of course; I don't mind at all.' And for the duration of about two weeks, I should say, we would eat our lunch together in one of the parks near the Congressional Library. Afterward I found out that he was a member of the Japanese Embassy in Washington, D.C.

"One afternoon, after we had finished our work at the library, he brought some of his friends from the embassy. They talked to my uncle and to my mother for a long time about certain conditions existing in the world. From that time I shall always remember that all minority groups probably have a kindred feeling because of the fact that although their color or nationality may be different, there is a bond in the fact that in certain areas they are oppressed and denied their rights. Thus they can feel or sympathize with the problems of other minority groups.

"I shall always feel an indebtedness to this young Japanese because of what he said and thought. He was indeed a gentleman of the old school."

In another interview conducted by Retha Lockett Swann and printed in the November 16, 1976, issue of *Insight,* Dr. Dykes shares her views on certain aspects of contemporary American life and the Seventh-day Adventist Church.

Q: "There has been much discussion about the black woman's relationship to the women's movement. Beyond the principle of equal pay for equal work, what are your feelings on this?"

A: "Black women should have accessibility to the freedoms that are available to white women. For the black Adventist woman any sought-after goals should be in keeping with Adventism."

Q: "As an English professor, how do you feel about the use of Ms. preceding a woman's name instead of the customary Miss or Mrs.?"

A: "It really depends on the purpose. My preference is Miss or Mrs. But maybe in a practical way I do prefer Ms. because there is prejudice at times toward single and married women."

Q: "What are your feelings on the ordination of women and the church's policy of selecting, in the majority of cases, only ordained ministers for key administrative positions?"

A: "There are some Adventists today who would not want a woman pastor. There was a Mr. Tibbs of Washington, D.C., who had a sister who was a minister in an SDA church in the Midwest. She was called a Bible reader, but she did the work of the minister and people praised her work. . . . Anna Knight is an example of a woman who traveled throughout the South and held many key positions. However, the home should not suffer. I might differ from some women's rights advocates on this point, but I feel that if a woman has young children her first duty is to them. She should not leave them to a nurse, baby-sitter, et cetera, unless she *has* to go out. When she does go out she should have the same opportunities as men. I think Adventists have followed the ways of the world in this matter. Women have proved themselves when given a chance, but preference is still given men. As you see, no women head any of the regional conferences."

Q: "Dr. Dykes, with divorce on the increase within society and also within the church, do you feel there is a need for a reassessment of the marital vows?"

A: "Marriage and morality is a problem of the last days. There is only one ground for divorce, but many Adventists are following the world and getting divorces for reasons such as incompatibility. There are some who are divorcing who have no sound reasons, and then they are remarrying."

Q: "Most Adventists seem to be apolitical. Do you feel that such isolation from the political mainstream has contributed to the insensitivity of many church members regarding current social problems?"

A: "I don't feel we follow the advice of Mrs. White in this area. We should become involved in politics, not to the extent that we forget religion or Adventism but, at the least, knowledgeable enough to vote on issues, providing there is no conflict between church and state. In the area of social problems, much more needs to be done in the way of social work, and more follow-up is needed. Where such work has been done it has been very effective in getting people interested in our message. The best way of attracting people, though, is to live the life."

Q: "How do you feel about the concept and slogan of black power?"

A: "Black youth have become black-conscious, and it is reflected in many areas, such as dress. If black youth, while attempting to assert themselves, are cruel or cause harm, they have gone overboard. I believe that the changes that have occurred within the church are a result of the actions of young people within society, and such activity affected the giving of more rights to the black Adventist membership."

Q: "Having written your Ph.D dissertation on Alexander Pope's influence in American literature, what role do you see literature (fiction), theater, and movies playing within the lives of Adventist young people and adults?"

A: "There are lessons to be learned from fiction. It can be relevant to our everyday living. Orwell's *1984* shows governmental intrusion into our private lives. Recently in the news we have seen the workings of the FBI and CIA in the private lives of individuals.

"The maturity of the person should be taken into consideration. If a child has a good foundation and training he will be able to cope with many kinds of experiences. The beggar lying on Abraham's bosom was not true, but there was a message there. Also the apostle Paul quotes from Ovid, a heathen writer.

"Plays that teach morals are fine. Students who take the Graduate Record Examination in English are required to know some plays. On Thirteenth

Sabbath we used to do little plays that were dramas. As far as attending the theater or movies, even though the play or picture may be acceptable, I feel we have to avoid the appearance of evil because we might influence negatively someone who is weak."

Q: "Dr. Dykes, you received what might be termed a classical education, having studied literature, languages such as Greek, Latin, French, and German, and mathematics throughout your school years. As an educator, what are your feelings about the kind of education students are receiving today?"

A: "I would not call the education I received classical, but I say it was more humanistic than what students are receiving now. The age in which we live puts the emphasis on practical learning, such as computer technology. Although technology is important and such technological skills are in high demand, I firmly believe that if the youth will take those subjects that develop the mind they will enjoy life more, and the other things they seek will come. I concur with Mrs. White that the hands should also be trained, but the mind is most important. Many people in prison have realized this by the self-training and education they have engaged in while locked up. Although the body was behind bars, the mind was not. As the poet Edward Dyer said: 'My mind to me a kingdom is.'"

Q: "At Oakwood you were known to dismiss your classes with the words 'audibility,' 'minimum essentials,' 'you students are excused.' What do these words mean?"

A: "Mrs. White says there should be minimum

essentials in all our schools. We should strive for perfection throughout all of them. Minimum essentials could be required and set by the General Conference, to ensure that when our students leave school they will have attained a certain level of proficiency."

Q: "During an era of affirmative action by our government in making attempts to integrate public institutions and positions at all levels within society, how do you feel about segregated Adventist institutions?"

A: "Prejudice within the church has affected the lives of many Adventists. I remember when some of the students and faculty at Oakwood tried to attend the white church in Huntsville and were refused entrance. Likewise, white schools were once discriminatory. So our black institutions exist for a reason. In addition, the black school offers our children something they can't seem to get from the white schools."

Q: "In 1945, *The Weekly Review*, of Huntsville, quoted you as saying in a commencement address, 'To be a Negro at this time demands love, patience, and loyalty.' Do you feel these demands have lessened any for the black man or woman today?"

A: "These demands apply to all times and to all peoples. Those who get to heaven will have love, patience, and loyalty to themselves, God, and others."

The Setting Sun

No matter how bright and beautiful the day, the sun must eventually set. Faculty, students, friends, and well-wishers gathered together at the new Sky Center Hotel near the Huntsville Airport, at 6:00 P.M., August 11, 1968, for the retirement recognition for Dr. Eva Beatrice Dykes.

There were many speeches and tributes, including recognition from the college president, Dr. Frank W. Hale, Jr., and the following letter from the head of her church.

"September 26, 1968

"Dear Dr. Dykes:

"What a wonderful life of service and dedication you have given to your church and the cause of education!

"Many of your former students and friends undoubtedly have expressed to you their appreciation and gratitude for what your life has meant to them. I want to add my voice to their chorus of tribute to a wonderful Christian lady and educator. In doing this, I know I also express the feelings of the church.

"You are much loved by your church for what you are and for what you have witnessed to others. In addition to the influence you have strongly exerted in the classroom and on the campus, some of us are much aware of the power of your pen and the numerous articles that you have contributed to various publications.

"Your writing has done much good. We thank you and God for what you have given to the church and humanity by your writing. We do hope and pray that your pen will continue to exert its character-shaping influence.

"May our dear Father always keep His hand over you, and continue to bless you richly until we all come to His kingdom in heaven.

"Very sincerely your brother,
"Robert H. Pierson"

The occasion had plenty of music, which was befitting a person who loved and appreciated music. The Faculty Women's Club, the Oakwood College Alumni Chapter, and the administration made presentations. Then the strains of the Oakwood College song rose as all joined in just prior to the benediction from Elder J. T. Stafford.

Forty-seven years of teaching, researching, writing, administering, were coming to a close. Her last assignment—to speak before the twenty Oakwood summer school graduates at ten o'clock the next Friday morning. On Sunday she would leave Huntsville for the Blue Ridge Mountains of Virginia.

Dr. Hale observed that her step had slowed down a bit in the past three years, but she was still a fast walker. "She just bounces across the campus. She's still very active.

"She still fixes her carrot juice and sleeps outdoors when the weather permits. In recent years they had built a screen porch, and if she could not sleep in the screen porch, she would at least sleep close to an open window."

"What will your retirement plans be, Dr. Dykes?"

Her answer: "I'd like to perhaps do some more research and criticism. I've got a long list, and it's just a matter of figuring out what hasn't been done by someone else before."

Someone asked her if workers should retire automatically at the age of 65, or if they should be asked to retire.

"In my opinion, one's physical and mental condition should be considered," she answered. "If a person's physical and mental condition have so deteriorated that one's usefulness is affected, I think a person should retire even before he reaches the age of 65.

"Consider the following pertinent statistics," she continued. "Gladstone at 80 engineered his greatest political coup and ruled England with a strong hand; Wellington planned and superintended fortifications at 80; Dr. Johnson's best work, *Lives of the English Poets*, was published at 78; Galileo was nearly 70 when he wrote on the laws of motion; Bismark was a power at 80; Longfellow, Whittier, and Tennyson wrote some of their best works after 70; Holmes, at 91, was known as the Supreme Court's great dissenter. I agree with Cicero who said that some men are like wine—age sours the bad and improves the good."

Now she headed for the countryside of Virginia. Her former pupil, Professor Nathaniel Ashby, had some years back, moved to the country and accepted a principalship at the Orange, Virginia, grade school. He and his wife, Lillian, had purchased a tract of land on the Orange-Albemarle side of Peter's Mountain, west of Gordonsville, Virginia, and remodeled an old home for retirement. Shortly thereafter, he died.

Mrs. Lillian Ashby, who had become a close friend of Eva over the years, and who had worked many years for local schools, invited her to come to her place. The quietness of the country and the beauty of the mountains, persuaded Dr. Dykes to purchase three acres from Mrs. Ashby, and prior to her retirement she had a new home built there.

"I wanted a quiet place to enjoy nature and stroll through the woods," she explained. "Many of my city friends like it here when they come to visit; many of them do not. They call this 'the sticks.' I love it. It's quiet here."

Visitors had to travel miles from the secondary State road to reach her new home. Twice they had to drive their cars across a swiftly moving though shallow stream. Small homes, many of them unkempt and unsightly, dotted the road.

Dr. Dykes's new home was at the end of the road—even a little past the end of it. A small wooded mountain rose rather sharply from her back door. She liked the rugged nature setting. Claiming she knew little about gardening or landscaping, she did not plan a garden or landscaping project.

Tucked away in her modest new home west of Gordonsville, she finally found time to read and to play the piano as much as she liked. During the first winter the electricity in her all-electric home didn't work, and she had to have a new chimney and fireplace installed. But she had time to read and study, and she continued writing for *Message.*

A Life Beautiful

Although many women made outstanding contributions to the academic and spiritual excellence at Oakwood, three special women surpassed them all. Eugenia Cunningham, Anna
Knight, and Eva Dykes were an awesome trio at
Oakwood College.

Eugenia Isabelle Cartwright Cunningham was
born in Stoneville, Mississippi. Sunday night,
Christmas, 1911, as she walked along the street with
an Adventist friend, Isabelle asked, "Do you celebrate
Christmas in your church?"

"No, Isabelle," came the answer. "The only day we
keep is the seventh-day Sabbath, Saturday. That is
the only day God commanded us to observe."

For a month this answer troubled her, and in
January, 1912, after studying with Elder J. G.
Dassent and other friends, she joined the Adventist
church in Natchez, Mississippi.

Eleven months later she ended up at Oakwood to
train to be a Bible instructor. She never accomplished
this objective, for the school administration
requested her to serve as matron of the orphanage,
then later matron of the dining hall, women's dean,
matron of the dining room again, manager of the
laundry, manager of the college store, and many other

responsible positions.

On March 18, 1948, when the college completed its new home for women students, they named it Cunningham Hall. Mother Cunningham stood on the steps during the dedication service. Speeches, songs, tears, and love witnessed to the fact that her life had been indeed a thing of beauty, and the building that honors her honors a person that was loved, known, and respected by hundreds of Oakwood students. Dr. Dykes penned the following words in the December 7, 1948, *Youth's Instructor:*

"Years ago a great poet wrote, 'A thing of beauty is a joy forever.' This world despite its ugliness and unhappiness and misery and suffering offers bright spots of beauty.

"There is the beauty of the skies at night when myriads of silver stars push through their sable curtain to sparkle in the silence of the heavens.

"There is the beauty of the sunset and the sunrise with their brilliant and delicate hues of crimson and gold and orange and blue and violet-purple.

"There is the beauty of green forest in spring and flaming wood in autumn.

"There is the beauty of the 'good' earth with its ever-changing carpets of white scintillating snow, green velvet grass, and rich, tawny, fallow ground.

"There is the beauty of music, of art, of poetry, of speech.

"But the greatest beauty of all is the beauty of character, the beauty of living, the beauty of life.

"Such beauty of character is exemplified in Eugenia Isabelle Cunningham, or as she is more familiarly known—'Mother Cunningham, Mother of Oakwood.'"

Dr. Dykes also admired another Mississippi girl,

Anna Knight, who worked at Oakwood. It was no accident that years later her beautiful life was memorialized in the new elementary building built at Oakwood College.

But the third member of the trio would also be memorialized for her work at Oakwood. Thousands of alumni from across the United States and around the world gathered at the college on April 20 to 22, 1973. They had listened to good preaching and had fellowship with their friends, but the highlight of the meeting was to honor a professor who had profoundly influenced each and every one of them, a teacher whose beautiful life had given spiritual dimensions to their lives.

They stood behind the ribbon as the new library with more than 600,000 volumes was dedicated to and named for Dr. Eva B. Dykes, who had served the school for more than thirty years.

At the opening ceremony, Dr. Frank W. Hale, former president of Oakwood, gave a special address. Then Dr. Garland J. Millet, former president and then associate secretary of the Department of Education of the General Conference, presented Dr. Dykes with a certificate of merit from the Department of Education. It is one of the highest awards given by this department of the church.

Following other speeches by the contractor, the builder, and the other presidents, Mr. Adel Warren, the business manager, passed the key of the library to the current president, Calvin B. Rock, who in turn, turned it over to Dr. Jannith Lewis, the librarian.

Mr. Thomas Hodges, mayor of Huntsville, praised the achievements of the institution. He mentioned how Oakwood had been a blessing to Huntsville. After cutting the ribbon, opening the doors, and inviting those present to enter into the modern building, Eva B. Dykes stepped forward. Followed by a great host of admirers, she, the mayor, and the presidents walked into the new library, which will serve Adventist youths as they enter its portals to learn and again depart to serve in various parts of the world.

Teacher of Teachers

The postman deposited several letters in the rural box. The one that caught her attention had come from Alabama. "Office of the President, Oakwood College," she read in the upper left-hand corner of the envelope. Good to hear from Dr. Hale, and find out how Oakwood is doing, she thought.

Eva ripped open the letter and scanned the page. "I, along with the leaders of Oakwood College, have voted to invite you to rejoin our staff. We know that you are enjoying your retirement, but we need you here at Oakwood to chair the English department."

Though she was enjoying the comfort of the country and the freedom of retirement, her college had sounded a new challenge for her. Eva was never one to turn down a call that meant service to her church and the cause of education. In September of 1970 she stood once more in the classroom, this time for three more years of full-time service. In 1973 she asked the administration to reduce her load, and she continued from 1973 to 1975 on a part-time basis.

It was during her second term at Oakwood that the new Eva B. Dykes Library was dedicated. She edited and published the *Pierian*, a paper that brought together a collection of original poems by students and fellow teachers like Florence Winslow and Irene Wakeham of the Oakwood English department.

She still had time to participate in musical activities, having once said, "Music has always given me more pleasure than anything else. If I have any gifts, I am more grateful for the gift of music than for any other."

In 1975 a letter from Washington, D.C., informed her that the General Conference would fly her to Vienna, Austria, where it would honor her along with several other outstanding women of the denomination. Dean Cooper wrote, when the denomination nominated Eva for its Outstanding Educators Award in Vienna, "The record of Dr. Dykes's contribution to Oakwood College is an illustrious and enviable one. She has served Oakwood with conspicuous excellence, with unflagging dedication, with extreme devotion, and with profound qualities of gentle greatness. . . . Dr. Dykes brought a spirit of true greatness to Oakwood College."

During 1976 the postman brought still another important letter. "From Wisconsin," she said to herself, puzzled. "Who in Wisconsin would be writing to me?" The return address indicated that it was from Dr. Geraldine Rickman, President, National Association of Black Professional Women in Higher Education. The letter invited Dr. Dykes to attend the charter meeting of the association at Wingspread, Johnson Foundation Conference Center in Racine, Wisconsin, on April 5. Accompanied by Mrs. Ruby Troy, an educator and wife of Dr. Owen Troy, the first Seventh-day Adventist black man to earn a Doctor of Theology, they attended this historic occasion.

The chairman introduced the honored guest to the hundreds of black women holding doctoral degrees that had assembled to discuss education and the woman's role in it. Some had their doctorates in education, some in science, others in English and the arts. They listened and admired the little lady as the chairman continued.

"We have in our midst a pioneer. Pioneers are special people. 'Firsts' are always difficult. We don't know that things can be done, that dreams can be fulfilled, that great accomplishments can be realized until somebody takes that first step and shows the way. Black women had never realized their full intellectual development and potential until this pioneer, Dr. Eva B. Dykes, fifty-five years ago dared to take the first step and show the way. We honor here the spirit of her dreams. We are proud that she can be our guest of honor at this charter meeting, and we grant her charter membership in this association as the first black woman to earn a Ph.D. in the United States."

The spontaneous and thunderous applause before and after her speech made her feel uncomfortable. But it was the fitting climax to a career of more than fifty years of distinguished teaching.

Now as professor emeritus, residing at Oakwood, she is a living monument of excellence, a legend in her own time.

H. D. Saulters wrote this about her, "I enjoy building things with wood. There have been a few items that I have constructed from wood and, when completed, I enjoyed seeing them placed where they served in some useful function. You are a builder also. You have been building minds. Unlike objects of wood, minds are not completely finished and then put to some useful task. The training that you have given to the minds of hundreds of young men and women has set in motion thinking powers that are ever growing broader and deeper.

"What joy can be yours as you lay aside your regular teaching duties and see many of your former students pushing forward and making strides in their journey throughout this life."

Lela M. Gooding ends her fifty-one-page research project by eulogizing her subject, "In a century that will survive in history through people like Mary McLeod Bethune and Martin Luther King, Jr., Malcolm X and Jessie Jackson, hers has been a quiet, almost uneventful life, but she deserves her place in the pantheon.

"Committed to a policy of refusal to retaliate, she nevertheless managed to play an aggressive role in the improvement of several thousand black people. As a black person, as a woman, as an academician, she has been a trailblazer. She will be remembered."

President Millet said of her, with tongue in cheek, "Dr. Dykes is a lamplighter. Those who know her want to emulate her, except in sleeping in the open air summer and winter."

Elder Louis B. Reynolds closed his article on her by observing, "When God has put an impossible dream in our hearts . . . He means to help us fulfill it. Eva Dykes believed this to be true, when as a young woman, she heeded the call to prepare herself to help others and to attain the highest competence in order to do it. Through the years God has given her many other dreams of specific tasks He wanted her to do.

"'It is when we resist God,' she says, 'that we remain nothing. When we submit to Him, whatever the sacrifice or hardship, we can become with His help far more than we dare dream.'"

Epilogue
August 13, 1893—October 29, 1986

The American flag outside the library that bears her name at Oakwood college flew at half mast. Just down the road, groups of people made their way to the Oakwood church in the peaceful afternoon sunlight. Among the mourners were educators and administrators, the full college choir, family members and old friends, church officers and members, and former and current students. All were conscious of the passing greatness. They had come to say goodbye to the legendary lady whose life had defined an era.

Many eulogies and speeches were made. Jannith Lewis, director of the Eva B. Dykes Library, traced the career of this devoted teacher. She ended by saying, "She was dynamic, inspiring, exacting, tireless, an excellent role model. She used Jesus Christ as her model. She was a great 'little giant,' small in stature but large in heart."

The bronze-tone casket was slipped into the back of a black hearse. Police escorts revved their motorcycles. Other cars fell into line. The procession moved slowly away, glass and chrome glittering in the afternoon sun.

Dr. Eva B. Dykes was leaving her beloved Oakwood for the last time.